MOUNTAIN BIKING

North Lake Tahoe's

BEST TRAILS

By Carol Bonser
and R. W. Miskimins

MOUNTAIN
BIKING
P R E S S™

FINE EDGE
Productions

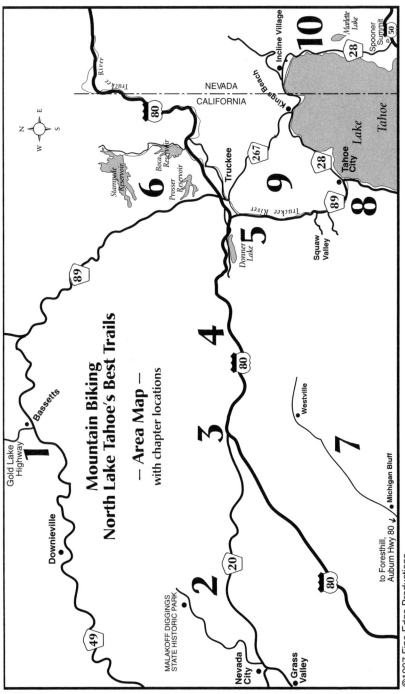

Mountain Biking
North Lake Tahoe's Best Trails

— Area Map —
with chapter locations

©1997 Fine Edge Productions

Mountain Biking
North Lake Tahoe's
Best Trails

Edited by Don and Réanne Douglass
Book design, layout, and digital cartography by Sue Irwin
Original maps by Carol Bonser and R.W. Miskimins
Cover photo courtesy of Incline Village & Crystal Bay Visitors Bureau
Back cover photo courtesy of Mammoth Mountain Bike Park
Inside photos by R.W. Miskimins, Bette E. Miskimins, and Carol Bonser

Important Disclaimer

Mountain biking is a potentially dangerous sport, and the rider or user of this book accepts a number of unavoidable risks. Trails have numerous natural and man-made hazards; they are generally not signed or patrolled, and they change with time and conditions.

While substantial effort has been made to provide accurate information, this guidebook may inadvertently contain errors and omissions. Any maps in this book are for locator reference only. They are not to be used for navigation. Your mileages will vary from those given in this book. Contact land managers before attempting routes to check for suitability and trail conditions.

The authors, editors, contributors, publishers, distributors, and public and private land managers accept no liability for any errors or omissions in this book or for any injuries or losses incurred from using this book.

Library of Congress Cataloging-in-Publication Data

Bonser, Carol.
    Mountain biking North Lake Tahoe's best trails / by Carol Bonser
and R.W. Miskimins.
        p.   cm.
    Includes index.
    ISBN 0-938665-40-5
        1. All terrain cycling–Tahoe, Lake, Region (Calif. and Nev.)–
    –Guidebooks.   2. Bicycle trails–Tahoe, Lake, Region (Calif. and
    Nev.)–Guidebooks.   3. Tahoe, Lake, Region (Calif. and Nev.)–
    –Guidebooks.   I. Miskimins, R. W. (Ray W.)   II. Title.
    GV1045.5.T16B65   1997
    917.94′38–dc21   97-15307
                                                                        CIP

TABLE OF CONTENTS

Riding high above Lake Tahoe

Acknowledgments

Carol Bonser wishes to thank the following people for their help and support throughout the creation of this guidebook. Mike Peart, who willingly explored with me the miles of trails described in this book, my brother, Gordon, who kept my mountain bike running for another summer of riding in the Sierra, and the rest of my family for their continued support. Thanks to all the "Sunday Riders" who have continued to support our ride program and offer encouragement to finish this second book. Special thanks to those of you whom Mike and I met out on the trail who shared with us some of your favorite rides so that others can enjoy them too. And last, thanks to Don and Réanne Douglass for asking me to write the original manuscript and supplying the extra motivation I needed to finish it, and to Sue Irwin for her help in readying the manuscript.

R. W. (Ray) Miskimins wishes to think his family for their constant support and assistance through this and many other projects over the years. His wife, Bette, has been extremely helpful with this North Lake Tahoe guidebook, providing new photographs and many hours of critical proofreading. Finally, thanks must be extended to the employees of Great Basin Bicycles in Reno, Nevada, for their willingness to help in any and all facets of the work of putting together this book.

Foreword

Many changes have occurred in the Lake Tahoe area since Carol Bonser wrote her first book on this region nearly a decade ago. Since that time, there have been highways built, bridges collapsed, forests burned, roads washed away, campgrounds expanded, and housing developments carved out of former wildlands.

Mountain Biking North Lake Tahoe's Best Trails is an all-new version of Carol's best-seller on this area. Ray Miskimins, author of numerous books and owner of Great Basin Bicycles in Reno, joins with Carol Bonser to provide updated trail descriptions, maps, and photos. In all, over 60 pages have been added to the earlier book, including new computer-generated maps and Ray's essays on bicycle maintenance, mountain biking skills, and roadside repairs. Ridden, researched, and written by experts who live near Lake Tahoe, this book should help its readers enjoy all the great riding the area has to offer.

Special Considerations

Mountain Biking North Lake Tahoe's Best Trails covers the Tahoe National Forest, parts of the Toiyabe National Forest and the northern portion of the Lake Tahoe Basin Management Unit. The National Forest within this area starts in the foothills at 2,000 feet, rising to nearly 10,000 in the mountains with wide ranges in climate and weather conditions.

This guidebook does not show all of the rides within each area. Part of the fun is discoveries you make while on the trail. Ride with your eyes wide open all the time!

1. Courtesy. Know and follow the IMBA Rules of the Trail (see Appendix A). Extend courtesy to all other trail users and follow the golden rule. The trails and roads in these areas are used by fishermen, hunters, loggers and hikers, who all feel proprietary about the use of the trails. Remember that mountain bikers are newcomers.

2. Preparations. Plan your trip carefully by developing a check list. Know your abilities and your equipment. Prepare to be self-sufficient at all times. If you plan to camp, be sure to read the warnings at the beginning of the chapters. Many of the campgrounds shown on the Tahoe National Forest are "undeveloped sites" which means that treated drinking water may not be available. Bring gallons of water with you from home to reduce the amount of stream water you'll have to treat (boiled for five minutes or filtered) before you can drink it. Regular maintenance and a careful pre-ride checkup for your bike can save a lot of grief from a breakdown 10 or 15 miles from civilization. (See the Appendix for discussions of bike maintenance and tools to carry.)

3. Mountain Conditions.
• Sun: Many of the high country rides travel over granite rocks which, in terms of reflected light, you can compare to riding across a snowfield. Protect your skin against the sun's harmful rays. Use sunscreen with a rating of 15 or more. Don't forget your eyes! Wear sunglasses with 100 UV protection. Clear lenses are also available with 100 UV protection. Avoid glass lenses!
• Low Humidity: Start each trip with a minimum of 2 full water bottles, or more. Gallons of water may not be sufficient for really hot weather. Force yourself to drink, whether or not you feel thirsty. Un-

treated drinking water may cause Giardiasis or other diseases. Carry water from a known source, or treat it.

• Variations in Temperature: Never travel to the high country without being prepared for afternoon thundershowers. It is not uncommon to get a brief hailstorm in midsummer! Carry extra clothing —a windbreaker, gloves, stocking cap, and use the multilayer system so you can adjust according to conditions. Keep an eye on changing cloud and wind conditions.

• Wind: Wind can deplete your energy. Sluggish or cramping muscles and fatigue indicate the need for calories. Carry high-energy snack foods such as granola bars, dried fruits and nuts to maintain strength and warmth, and add clothing layers as the temperature drops or the wind increases.

• Know how to deal with dehydration, hypothermia, altitude sickness, sunburn or heatstroke. Be sensitive at all times to the natural environment–the land can be frightening and unforgiving. If you break down, it will take you longer to walk out than it took you to ride in! Check with your local Red Cross, Sierra Club, or mountaineering textbooks for detailed survival information.

Ride stopper: the taco'd wheel

4. Pack Animals and Horses. Many trails mentioned in this guide are used by recreational horse riders. Some horses are spooked easily, so make them aware of your presence well in advance of the encounter.

If you come upon horses moving toward you, yield the right-of-way, even when it seems inconvenient. Carry your bike to the downhill side and stand quietly, well off the trail in a spot where the animals can see you

Trailhead parking lot

clearly. A startled horse can cause serious injuries both to an inexperienced rider and to itself.

If you come upon horses moving ahead of you in the same direction, stop well behind them. Do not attempt to pass until you have alerted the riders and asked for permission. Then, pass as quietly as you can on the downhill side of the trail. It is *your* responsibility to ensure that such encounters are safe for everyone!

5. Respect the Environment. Minimize your impact on the natural environment. *Remember, mountain bikes are not allowed in Wilderness Areas, on the Pacific Crest Trail, and in certain other restricted areas.* Ask, when in doubt. You are a visitor. Leave plants and animals alone, historic and cultural sites untouched. Stay on established roads and trails, and do not enter private property. Follow posted instructions and use good common sense. Note: If you plan to camp within the National Forest, you need a Campfire Permit to have a fire or use a stove outside of a campground. For information on permits, regulations and seasonal fire closures, contact the Tahoe National Forest Service at (916) 265-4531. To report fires, call (702) 883-5995—a 24-hour interagency dispatch center.

6. Control and Safety. Keep your mountain bike in control at all times. Guard against excessive speed. Avoid overheated rims and brakes on long or steep downhill rides. Lower your center of gravity by lowering your seat on downhills. Lower your tire pressure on rough or sandy stretches. (See the Appendix for a description of basic mountain biking skills.) Avoid opening weekend of hunting season (ask local sporting goods stores which areas are open to hunting). Don't ride by yourself in remote areas. Carry first aid supplies and bike tools for emergencies.

7. First Aid and Safety. Carry first aid for your body as well as for your bike. Several companies market first aid kits specifically designed for cyclists. If you have allergies be sure to bring your medicine, whether it's for pollen or bee stings. Also be aware of the following:

There are *black bears* out and about. Food seems to cause the most problems, so a clean camp is advised. *Rattlesnakes* can be startling and are dangerous at close range, but they are usually noisy and retreat readily. Snakes are most often seen in the lower elevations, close to a water source, hidden in the rocks. Most snake bites are reported in April, May and early June when the snakes lie in the sun trying to warm up. Later on in the summer, they will be hiding in the shade, and you probably won't see them. *Mosquitoes and deerflies* are more of an annoyance than a true health hazard. If the mosquitoes like you, carry insect repellent when riding, especially during the months of May through July. Avoid *poison oak*. Usually found in this area at 4,000 feet and below, this three-leaved plant—sometimes a bush, sometimes a vine—has an oil that causes rashes with blistering one to five days after contact. Avoid direct contact with any part of the plant, contact with an animal that's brushed against it, contact with clothing or gloves that have touched it, or inhalation of smoke from a burning plant. Wash immediately to prevent or lessen the rash. For more severe cases see your doctor.

8. Maps & Navigation. Everyone who enjoys exploring by mountain bike should know how to read a map and use a compass. The maps in this book are designed to be used with National Forest Maps and U.S. Geological Survey Maps (USGS topo maps). A "legal description" (location) is given for the starting point of each area. For example, T20N, R16E, Section 30 is the location of the Bear Valley Campground, a good place to camp and ride. Maps are made up of grids. Across the top and bottom of the Tahoe National Forest Map are the numbers R8E to R18E, for Range 8 East to Range 18 East. Vertically on the left and right are T13N to T22N, for Township 13 North to Township 22 North. Using the legal description for Bear Valley Campground, find where T20N and R16E cross, forming a large square made up of smaller squares, called sections. Each section is numbered from 1-36. You should now have no problem locating Bear Valley Campground within Section 30. *Warning: Not all the roads on the USFS maps are on the guidebook maps, and not all the roads found on the maps in this guidebook are on the USFS maps!*

The handiest maps to use while riding are the USGS topo maps, 7.5 minute series. These maps tend to be the most recent and have most of the newer roads on them. Everything you learned about the legal descriptions is the same for the topo maps, the squares are just larger. Each section of the maps, no matter which one you are using, represents one square mile.

Another hint! Have you ever noticed trees in the forest with yellow tags nailed onto them? These tags are called K-Tags. On each K-Tag is one complete Township with 36 sections. On the top or bottom of the tag will be the Township and Range numbers. Then there should be one nail hole in a section square indicating the section you're in. Look on your map and you can quickly find out where you are!

It's easy to get lost. Before you leave on a trip, tell someone where you're going, when you expect to return, and what to do in case you don't return on time. When you are more than six hours overdue ask them to contact the appropriate County Sheriff's Department, giving full details about your vehicle and your trip plans. En route, keep track of your position on your trip map(s); record the time you arrive at a known point on the map. Look back frequently in the direction from which you came, in case you need to retrace your path.

Don't be afraid to turn back when conditions change or if the going is rougher than you expected. In case of emergency while you're in this area, dial 911.

9. Trailside Bike Repair. Minimum equipment: pump, spare tube, patches, 2 tubes of patch glue, Allen wrenches, chain tool, spoke wrench, and a 6" adjustable wrench. Tools may be shared with others in your group.

Correct inflation, wide tires, and avoiding rocks will prevent most flats. Grease, oil, and proper adjustment will prevent almost all mechanical failures. (Please see the Appendix for more information on caring for and repairing your bike.)

High Sierra trail riding

CHAPTER 1

Sierra Buttes

A visit to Sierra Buttes should appear on every mountain bike riders "must do" list! The Sierra Buttes are gigantic, jagged, rocky pinnacles that push straight up over 2,000 feet from the surrounding forest lands. They can be seen from miles away and form a strong contrast to the more gentle northern Sierra Nevada. The forest land below the Buttes, known as the Lakes Basin Recreation Area, has an incredible amount of area to explore by mountain bike. Nearby lakes provide swimming, fishing, windsurfing and water skiing and there are many places to camp. Plan to spend at least a couple of days, but you won't be disappointed if you take an entire week's vacation here.

Sierra Buttes and the Lakes Basin are located on the Gold Lake Highway, named after Gold Lake, the largest lake in the area. *From the Bay Area or Sacramento:* Take Interstate 80 east to Auburn and go north on Highway 49, which travels through the Gold Country and then climbs back into the Sierra Nevada. About 16 miles east of Downieville, at the small town of Bassetts, turn north on the Gold Lake Highway. *From Lake Tahoe:* Go north on Highway 89 to Sierraville. Turn left, staying on Highway 89 (49 and 89 at this point), and follow the signs to Quincy. Five miles farther turn left on Highway 49 and follow the signs to Downieville. You will drive over Yuba Pass before dropping down the west side to get your first glimpse of the Sierra Buttes. When you reach Bassetts, turn right (north) on the Gold Lakes Highway. To get a geographic perspective of the area, just after you turn stop and check out the posted maps for the Downieville Ranger District of the Tahoe National Forest.

The rides in this chapter all start from different campgrounds or intersections along Gold Lake Highway. You can either drive to the starting points, or look at the map to see how much pavement riding is involved from your campsite to the start. The Pacific Crest Trail

The Sierra Buttes

(closed to mountain bikes) runs north-south along the edge of this area. Fortunately, there are plenty of 4-wheel drive roads that parallel the trail, so this closure doesn't cause much of a problem in planning rides.

Emergency: Dial 911. Sierra County Sheriff: (916) 289-3234. U.S. Forest Service, Downieville Ranger District: (916) 288-3231. Pay phones are located at Bassetts and Sardine Lake Resort.

Campgrounds: Sardine and Salmon Creek are full-service USFS campgrounds with water, tables, fire rings and vault toilets. There are also five camping areas that the Forest Service calls "undesignated" or "undeveloped" campgrounds. These all have vault toilets, but they may or may not have tables and they probably offer only stream or lake water for drinking. All water from these areas should be boiled or filtered before drinking. Due to the popularity of this region, camping is primarily limited to the campgrounds.

Seasons: June through October.

Nearest Services: There is a store and a gas station in Bassetts, but you should bring the majority of your supplies from home. The nearest bike shops are in Truckee or Grass Valley—both a few hours away—so bring all your tools and extra bike parts.

In addition to camping, there are cabins for rent at Sardine Lakes Resort. These are old wooden structures that have been refurbished, and Sardine Lakes Resort is a small, beautiful resort to visit on your tour. Boats can be rented, and there is a Dining Room that serves delicious gourmet family-style dinners (a great treat after a hard day of riding!). For more information on Sardine Lake Resort, call (916) 862-1196.

#1   Upper Sardine Lake

Level of Difficulty: Short intermediate level ride. The road is rough and rocky, the ride moderately technical; beginners may prefer to walk. But don't miss this one, even if you hike instead of ride. The view is worth the effort it takes to get there!
Mileage: 2.5 miles out and back.
Elevation: 5,700 ft. to 6,000 ft.
Topo Maps: Haypress Valley and Sierra City 7.5 min., or Sierra City 15 min.
Trailhead Location: Sardine Lake Campground, T20N, R12E, Section 3.

0.0 mile - Beginning at Sardine Lake Campground, ride toward Lower Sardine Lake (southwest) and go past the picnic area to

Meadow singletrack

the entrance of Sardine Lake Resort (0.3 mile). Turn right on the road that is just to the right of the resort—it is narrow and paved for the first 100 feet before turning to dirt. Follow the rocky, dirt road 1 mile farther up to Upper Sardine Lake. On the way up you will be treated to a view down to Lower Sardine Lake with the Sierra Buttes in the background. But the view gets even better when you get to Upper Sardine Lake where the Buttes rise 2,500 feet straight up from the water! Be sure to search for the lookout tower perched on the rocks. Upper Sardine Lake is a fun place for an early morning or early evening ride. Plan to spend some time just enjoying the sights.

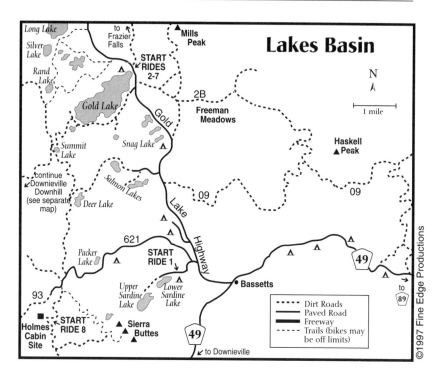

#2 Mills Peak Lookout

Level of Difficulty: Most beginners in good physical condition could handle this one. With only 900 feet of elevation gain, this is an easy ride compared to most lookout hill climbs.

Mileage: Out and back, total of 7.6 miles.

Elevation: 6,400 ft. to 7,300 ft.

Topo Maps: Gold Lake and Clio 7.5 min., or Sierra City 15 min.

Trailhead Location: T12N, R12E, Section 16—Gold Lake Campground, located about 6 miles north of the Sardine Lake Campground turnoff. There are two ways to access the campground—the old entrance at the picnic area and a new gravel road 0.3 mile farther south.

0.0 mile - From the campground, ride south on the Gold Lake Highway. 0.6 mile - Turn left on the dirt road with a sign that reads: *Mills Peak Lookout 3 1/4 miles.* 1.3 miles - Ignore a road that enters from the left. 1.6 miles - Turn left here. You are passing through private land, so stay on the main road. As you leave the private land, the road begins to climb and makes the final ascent to the lookout. There are several junctions, but just stay on the main road which continues uphill. 3.8 miles - From the top you can see Mohawk Valley in the distance to the northeast, the high point of Mills Peak to the southeast, and the jagged pinnacles of Sierra Buttes to the southwest. When you have finished exploring follow your tracks back, enjoying the downhill. For a longer loop see Ride #3 below.

#3   Haskell Peak Loop

Level of Difficulty: Strong beginners and up. Suitable for all riders who have the endurance to handle the distance. Not at all technical—all of the road surfaces are either good dirt or gravel.
Mileage: 18.5 miles round trip from Gold Lake (the ride is reduced to 17 miles if you choose to start at Snag Lake).
Elevation: 6,400 ft. to 7,720 ft.
Water: Carry all you think you will need. You will pass a few creeks along the way, but I would not count on them as a year-round source. Be sure to filter or treat all water you take from mountain streams.
Topo Maps: Gold Lake and Clio 7.5 min., or Sierra City 15 min.
Trailhead Location: T12N, R12E, Section 16 (Gold Lake—see Ride #2) or, as an option, Section 21 (Snag Lake).

0.0 mile - From Gold Lake camping area, follow the directions in Ride #2 for the first 1.6 miles. Then, instead of turning toward the lookout you continue straight ahead and shortly arrive at an intersection (1.7 miles). Head straight on Forest Road 28.

Optional Start: From Snag Lake Campground, go right on Gold Lake Highway for 0.2 mile. Turn left on the road to Mills Peak and continue to an intersection 0.8 mile farther (1.0 miles total). Turn right onto Forest Road 28. If you take this option, be sure to adjust your mileage by subtracting 0.7, since all figures are given from here on for the trip starting at Gold Lake.

Once you are on Forest Road 28 (1.7 miles from Gold Lake or 1.0 miles from Snag Lake), follow the signs to Church Meadows and Haskell Peak. 2.3 miles - Turn right at the road signed: *Dead End Road, Not Maintained 12N11, Church Creek Meadows.* You will ride past large Freeman Meadow, with Church Creek running through it. 3.9 miles - Stay left at the intersection. The road begins to gradually climb. 4.1 miles - At another intersection, continue straight ahead. From here on you will pass several intersections, but just remember to stay on the main road that climbs to the saddle just west of Haskell Peak. 6.3 miles - The climbing is over and you are on the saddle. As you turn the corner you get a good look at the rocky top of Haskell Peak (elev. 8,107 ft.).

You can detour over to the base of the rocks, but you will have to hike to get to the top of the peak. After you've enjoyed the view, prepare yourself for the next eight miles—almost all downhill! 6.8 miles - Continue down the main road to the three-way intersection. 7.1 miles - Turn left.

8.2 miles - Turn right and continue downhill. From here the road begins to wind its way around the ridge. You climb a little and then head downhill. The road is now marked *Forest Road 09*, and it has arrows and orange diamonds denoting a ski and snowmobile route. Stay on Forest Road 09, and you should have no problem keeping to the route even though there are logging roads everywhere! Watch for indications of active logging, and ride with caution. 12.3 miles - You cross Howard Creek and then have to climb a bit. Winding around the ridge, you are treated to another great view of Sierra Buttes in the distance. From here it is all downhill to Gold Lake Highway. 15.2 miles - At Gold Lake Highway turn right and ride back to your starting point - 1.6 miles to Snag Lake or 3.3 miles to the Gold Lake Campground.

#4 Frazier Falls Picnic Ride

Level of Difficulty: Easy, on a wide, well-travelled dirt road. The ride out and back to Frazier Falls is suitable for families or those looking for a short ride and a good place to picnic. It is about as flat as a mountain bike ride can be, with only 200 feet of elevation change. The longer loop is still an easy ride but not recommended for children because you have to ride on the Gold Lake Highway for 1.8 miles.
Mileage: 3.6 miles; loop ride 5.4 miles.
Elevation: 6,200 ft. to 6,400 ft. Longer loop 6,200 ft. to 6,500 ft.
Topo Maps: Gold Lake 7.5 min., or Sierra City 15 min.
Trailhead Location: T12N, R12E, Section 16 (Gold Lake Campground—see Ride #2).

0.0 mile - From the Gold Lake camping area, ride out to Gold Lake Highway. Look across the highway for a dirt road; ride across when it is safe and continue out the dirt road. The ride is slightly downhill as you make your way past rocky outcroppings and small meadows. 1.8 miles - You arrive at the Frazier Falls trailhead and picnic area. Park your bike and take the short hike over to the falls (a photo opportunity!). Enjoy your picnic, then ride back to Gold Lake for a swim.

For the longer loop, you can continue ahead on the main road (it soon turns to pavement), turn left at 2.5 miles and tie back into Gold

Lake Highway. 3.6 miles - Turn left onto the highway and ride back to Gold Lake. This is a nice loop, but much of it on paved roads!

#5   Summit Lake

Level of Difficulty: Intermediate because of the technical rocky sections. Beginners can do part of the ride, out to Little Gold Lake and back, to practice riding on rocks.
Mileage: 8 miles to Summit Lake and back, 10 miles if you detour to all of the other lakes.
Elevation: 6,407 ft. to 7,000 ft.
Water: The nearest treated water is back at Salmon Creek Campground. Be sure to filter or treat all water you take from lakes and streams.
Topo Maps: Gold Lake 7.5 min., or Sierra City 15 min.
Trailhead Location: T12N, R12E, Section 16 (Gold Lake Campground—see Ride #2).

0.0 mile - From the Gold Lake camping area, turn right (south) onto Gold Lake Highway. 0.8 mile - Turn right on the gravel road that goes to the boat launching area. There is a dirt route connecting the camping area to the boat launch, but we found the short ride on the pavement a good way to warm up for the next section of the ride. 1.2 miles - Ride past the turnoff to the stable and the boat ramp, and continue to the end of the gravel road. Look to your left for a sign: *Squaw Lake 1 mile - Jeep Campground 1 1/4 miles - Little Gold Lake 2 miles - Summit Lake 3 miles.* There is room for a few cars here; this area and the nearby boat ramp parking lot are alternative places to start this ride.

From here on the road gets rough! Some sections are quite rocky and look like streambeds, but never for very long. Be on the lookout for horses, because the Pack Station runs five trips a day on busy weekends. The horses seem accustomed to mountain bikes, but don't forget that many of the riders have very little experience. If you see a group of horseback riders, warn them of your presence, then slow down to a snail's pace or dismount until they pass.

2.0 miles - On your left is the turnoff to Squaw Lake, about a half a mile uphill (250 feet elevation gain). Detour up to the lake now, or stop on your way back. (The mileage given below does not include any of these lake detours.) 2.7 miles - On your left is the turnoff to Little Gold Lake, which you can see through the trees. 3.0 miles - Ride southeast to the far end of Gold Lake to some great campsites. Continue until you reach the *Private Land* sign and the cable across the road. Take a left turn, and begin the uphill part of the ride. The next section winds up and away from Gold Lake, passing a cabin, then crosses the Pacific Crest Trail. Stay on the main road to the top of the ridge—a good climb.

If you start to tire or have to push your bike, just remember that it is only 1 mile to the top. After you crest the ridge the road goes downhill to Summit Lake. 4.0 miles - You have reached the end of this ride. Summit Lake is off to the left, and you are at a major OHV Trail intersection. A right turn heads to Round Lake (see Ride #6); a left turn leads to Deer Lake and on out the ridge towards the Buttes. The road straight ahead takes you on the Downieville Downhill, Ride #7. When you are through exploring, either follow the directions for Ride #6, or turn around and enjoy a fast downhill back to Gold Lake!

#6 Round Lake Loop

Level of Difficulty: Strong intermediate or better. This is a scenic ride for people who don't mind pushing their bikes through some of the rough spots. Be prepared for a mile of steady climbing, rocky sections and some singletrack.
Mileage: 9 miles.
Elevation : 6,400 ft. to 7,320 ft.
Topo Maps: Gold Lake 7.5 min., or Sierra City 15 min.
Trailhead Location: T12N, R12E, Section 16 (Gold Lake Campground—see Ride #2).

0.0 mile - Start from Gold Lake camping area and follow the directions for Ride # 5 for the first 4 miles to Summit Lake. 4.0 miles - Turn right at the intersection. The road climbs a bit more before you reach an open ridge with a great view of Gold Lake. The OHV road you are riding crosses the Pacific Crest Trail in several places. 5.3 miles - Turn right, staying on the east side of the ridge. (The road to the left goes to Oakland Pond.) A short distance farther you pass a sign: *Round Lake 3/4 mile - Silver Lake 1 3/4 mile: Lakes Basin Campground 2 3/4 mile.* 6.0 miles - On the edge of the ridge you are treated to a view of Round Lake and Long Lake, with Mt. Elwell in the background. The next section is a steep downhill that many prefer to walk.

6.2 miles - You arrive at the overlook above Round Lake. There is a plaque that tells about a 400-foot mine shaft that was dug here shortly before World War I, when the ore was valued at $1.05 a ton! It is hard to believe that there was that much activity at such a remote place as this, so long ago. This spot is also the intersection with the

Windy day at Gold Lake

trail to Silver Lake. From this point you should pull out your map and plan the rest of your journey. There are trails and old roads connecting all of the lakes. A nice loop option is to ride out to Silver Lake, Cub Lake, Little Bear Lake, Big Bear Lake, and then tie into the road on the Round Lake Loop.

To complete the Round Lake Loop, continue on the main trail that turns into a narrow old road. Around the corner you pass an old shelter, and then the road starts downhill. This next section is a lot of fun as you go through rocky areas and back into the forest. Be on the lookout for hikers. The roadbed is wide enough to pass them safely, but be sure to let them know you are coming. 7.5 miles - The old road intersects with the trail to Bear Lakes. (This is where you will reenter if you take the optional ride out to the other lakes.) 7.8 miles - The old road ends at a trailhead parking area. There is a good map of the Lakes Basin area that you may want to look at if you don't have a topo map. Ride out to Gold Lakes Highway, turn right, and continue back to the Gold Lake Campground.

#7 Downieville Downhill

This is a ride we heard about from a group of riders we met while exploring the area. The route is a little complicated; the first time you ride, take the 7.5 min. USGS topo maps along and you should have no problem finding your way to Downieville. You will need to arrange a shuttle or leave a car somewhere near the town of Downieville. There is very little parking in Downieville, so you might find it easier to have someone meet you just outside of town along Highway 49. (There are good swimming holes on the North Fork of the Yuba River.)

Start of the Downieville Downhill

Level of Difficulty: Experienced riders only. Losing over 4,000 feet of elevation can be exhilarating, but it is also tiring. Be sure you have a good bike with an excellent set of brakes.
Mileage: 16 miles one way (rarely ridden out and back!).
Elevation: 6,407 ft. to 7,000 ft. to 2,899 ft.
Water: This ride takes you along several creeks. Be sure to filter or treat all water you take from the streams.
Topo Maps: Gold Lake, Sierra City and Downieville 7.5 min. are the best. Otherwise use Sierra City and Downieville 15 min. maps.
Trailhead Location: At Gold Lake Campground (see directions in Ride #2).

0.0. mile - From Gold Lake camping area, follow Ride #5 the first 4 miles to Summit Lake. 4.0 miles - When you reach Summit Lake continue on the main OHV trail that goes straight ahead. Follow the signs to Gold Valley and Pauley Trail. (On some maps this road is called the Summit Lake Trail.) As you drop down the west side of the ridge, it's an all downhill ride into Gold Valley 1,100 feet below. You ride past several intersections, many of them leading to old mines. Stay on the main road and keep following the signs to Gold Valley and Pauley Trail. 7.2 miles - When you enter Gold Valley, the road turns south down the valley. After crossing Pauley Creek, you arrive at an intersection with the road going to Smith Lake, which is located 0.7 mile west of this point. Continue to the southern end of Gold Valley on the Pauley Creek Trail. 7.7 miles - As you leave the valley, the trail descends quickly into Pauley Creek Canyon. Continue on the trail as it follows the creek downstream.

9.4 miles - Pauley Creek Trail intersects with Butcher Ranch Trail (11E08). Stay to the right and continue to follow Pauley Creek. You have descended over 2,000 feet since you left Summit Lake, and the canyon walls are getting quite steep. Continue on the main trail that goes downhill. 11.4 miles - Stay to the right on the Third Divide Trail (11E07). Ride through the divide and continue downhill to Lavezzola Creek and Empire Ranch. Stay left on the main road that follows Lavezzola Creek, crosses it, and goes through the Second Divide back to Pauley Creek. From here just stay on the main road and follow all the signs to Downieville. Eventually you will be on road S514. 14.8 miles - When the dirt road ends, continue straight ahead on the paved road that takes you into Downieville. 15.6 miles - Turn left onto Highway 49 where either your car or a friend's car is waiting for you.

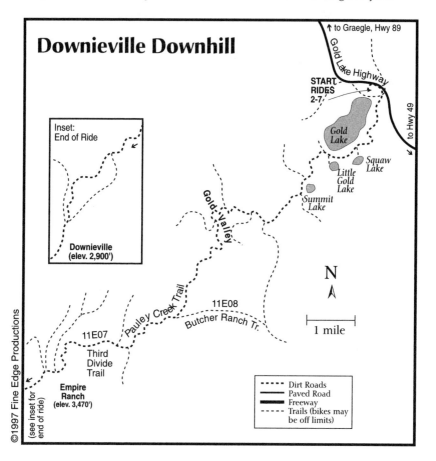

Downieville Downhill

#8 Sierra Buttes Lookout

Level of Difficulty: A difficult ride for advanced riders who like the challenge of a steep hill climb. Others may prefer to hike up the PCT instead.

Mileage: 7.5 miles out and back from Holmes Cabin. (For a longer ride, you can do 16 miles out and back from Packer Lake.)

Elevation: 6,773 ft. to 8,591 ft. from Holmes Cabin Site (6,224 ft. to 8,591 ft. from Packer Lake).

Water: None. Carry all you will need.

Topo Maps: Sierra City 7.5 min. or 15 min.

Trailhead Location: T20N, R12E, Section 5—the Holmes Cabin Site, or Packer Lake (see driving directions prior to ride description).

Most cyclists on mountain bikes think of lookouts as destination points for ultimate hill climbs and wild descents, and the Sierra Buttes Lookout is one of the toughest around. From the lakes below, you can see the Lookout Tower perched on the top of the highest pinnacle. This is not a route recommended for those afraid of heights. Once you arrive at the top of the road, you have three flights of steep narrow stairs (with guard rails!) to climb before reaching the tower. *Caution: Do not attempt to ride to the Sierra Buttes Lookout Tower unless you have good brakes! The downhill return is very steep, and the drop-offs are severe!* Some people prefer to walk up to the lookout rather than ride (push) up the OHV road to the top.

Going to Sierra Buttes Lookout is something everyone should do who has more than one day to spend in this area. To get to the trailhead follow the signs to Packer Lake. Ride or drive past Packer Lake on Forest Road 93. The road is paved, although quite narrow all the way to the top (suitable for mountain bikes, but not road bikes!).

From the top, turn left onto a dirt road and follow the signs to the lookout (3 miles). Stay on the main road and you will arrive at the Pacific Crest Trailhead, which is also the trailhead for the Lookout. If you decide to hike to the top, park your bikes here. (I would carry locks for stashing them behind trees somewhere.) Continue on by foot. If you to ride to the lookout continue on the gravel road that will take you to the OHV road to the top.

From here the road goes downhill and winds its way around the ridge. In the big left turn that goes around the ridge, you will see the old Holmes Cabin Site. If you are still driving, this is a good place to park so you get a little warm-up before you start the climb.

0.0 mile - From Holmes Cabin Site (8.5 miles from Packer Lake), continue out the gravel road, which turns into a dirt road. 1.2 miles - The OHV trailhead takes off to the left. (The road to the right is a wild downhill ending in Sierra City!). There is a sign at the Trailhead: *Sierra Buttes Lookout 1 1/4 miles - OHV Road ends 1 mile.* Now the climb begins! If it hasn't rained in a while the road surface will be quite loose, and you may find yourself pushing more than you think you should. The OHV road runs straight up the ridge, then pushes out into an open brushy area with no shade. It appears that this side of the Buttes burned off several years ago and hasn't grown back yet. The view into the North Yuba River Canyon 3,000 feet below is sensational! You can see the Pacific Crest Trail winding its way 7 miles down to Sierra City. After the road crosses the Pacific Crest Trail, it turns back into a forested area and continues the climb.

3.2 miles - The OHV road and the trail meet. There is a large sign that reads *No Vehicles Beyond This Point.* If you are here on a busy weekend, this is a good place to leave your bike. But if it isn't crowded, you might want to ride the last half mile to the top. Here the road narrows and has several hairpin turns with magnificent views. 3.7 miles - The road ends, and the stairway to the lookout begins. If it's clear when you visit the Lookout, you can see Mt. Shasta and Mt. Lassen far to the north. Closer and down below are Upper and Lower Sardine Lakes, Deer Lake and Upper Salmon Lake. The large lake to the south is Jackson Meadows Reservoir (see Chapter 3). Make your way down the stairs and back to your bike. *Caution: Be careful on the way down, especially the first three turns! Watch out for hikers!* The Lookout people told us they get over 100 visitors in the tower on busy summer days. Retrace your route back to your car.

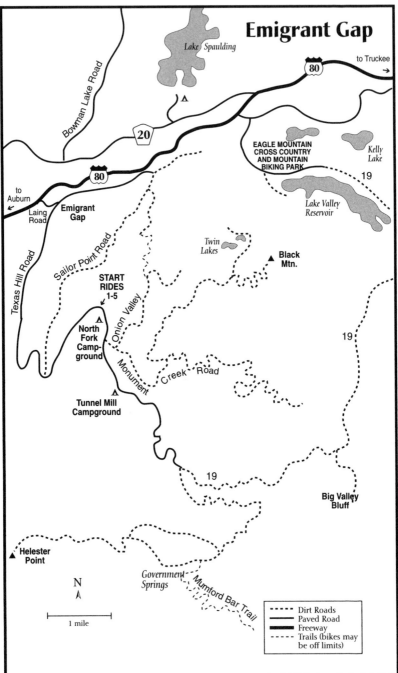

Emigrant Gap

Lake Spaulding

to Truckee →

80

20

EAGLE MOUNTAIN
CROSS COUNTRY
AND MOUNTAIN
BIKING PARK

Kelly
Lake

19

80

to
Auburn
←

Laing
Road

**Emigrant
Gap**

Lake Valley
Reservoir

Texas Hill Road

Bowman Lake Road

Sailor Point Road

Twin
Lakes

▲ **Black
Mtn.**

**START
RIDES
1-5**

Onion Valley

**North
Fork
Camp-
ground**

Monument

Creek Road

19

**Tunnel Mill
Campground**

19

**Big Valley
Bluff**

▲ **Helester
Point**

N

Government
Springs

Mumford Bar Trail

1 mile

········ Dirt Roads
────── Paved Road
━━━━━ Freeway
- - - - - Trails (bikes may
        be off limits)

©1997 Fine Edge Productions

CHAPTER 2

🚲

The Foothills

This chapter describes rides in the foothill country of the western slope of the Sierra Nevada Range within Tahoe National Forest. The elevation in the Emigrant Gap Area ranges from 5,000 to 6,000 feet; in the area of the Malakoff Diggings from 2,000 to 5,000 feet. At these lower elevations the season for mountain bike riding lasts longer than in the higher country. This is the chapter in which you can find rides for late fall and early spring, with some rides closed only during low elevation snowstorms.

EMIGRANT GAP

As you drive east from Auburn on Interstate 80, the Emigrant Gap area is one of the first sites with easy access to National Forest lands. To get to this area, take the Laing Road (Emigrant Gap) off-ramp, turn right (west) on Emigrant Gap Road. Soon, Emigrant Gap Road ends and becomes Texas Hill Road (narrow, paved FS19). The rides in this section all radiate from North Fork Campground on Texas Hill Road. Here, you ride through foothill canyons from 4,500 to 6,500 feet, following the many forks of the North Fork of the American River.

Trailhead Location: All rides start and end from North Fork Campground, T16N, R12E, Section 8.
Topo Maps: Blue Canyon, Cisco Grove, Duncan Peak, Westville, 7.5 min., or Emigrant Gap, Duncan Peak, 15 min.
Campgrounds: USFS Campgrounds North Fork and Tunnel Mill (a group campground) are located on Texas Hill Road. North Fork Campground has a water system.
Seasons: April through mid-November, depending on snow level.

31

Nearest Services: None at Emigrant Gap; bring all supplies with you. The closest town to the west is Colfax. To the east, Cisco Grove has small stores and gas stations. You can purchase major supplies in Truckee.

#1   Sailor Point Loop

Sailor Point Loop is part chip seal and part dirt. If you're looking for a winter ride in the snow, this loop is a good one to try, providing the snow is not too deep. The ride is described starting from North Fork Campground, but since it is a loop that goes through Emigrant Gap, it also can be started right at the Laing Road off-ramp at I-80.

Leisurely forest trail

Level of Difficulty: Intermediate. Climbing is done, for the most part, on broken chip seal; the dirt portions are rocky, but not very technical.
Mileage: 16 miles.
Elevation: 4,760 ft. to 5,410 ft.
Water: At North Fork Campground and at streams along the ride. Be sure to filter or treat all water you take from mountain streams.

0.0 mile - From North Fork Campground, turn left and ride up Texas Hill Road–part paved, part broken-up chip seal–back to Emigrant Gap. 7.0 miles - You pass Sailor Point Road on your right where the loop portion of the ride will end. Continue on the main road east, past the Laing Road off-ramp to Interstate 80 and past Carpenter Flat. When you reach the *Do not enter* sign for another freeway off-ramp at 8.0 miles, stay to the right. 8.2 miles - Turn right when the pavement ends. Continue past a few homes, then up a hill and across a PG&E ditch. Stay right at the next intersection. 10.0 miles - You come to a gate (closed in winter) and the start of Sailor Point Road. This road, a combination of dirt and river rock, goes down the oak and pine forest, climbing its way up onto a ridge. Follow the main road out the ridge; then the downhill begins. Sailor Point Road ends at 13.9 miles, which is also the end of the loop. Turn left on Texas Hill Road and continue on downhill back to the campground.

#2 Sawtooth Ridge Loop

Level of Difficulty: Intermediate or better. Beginners might want to drive to the top of the ridge at the 3.3 mile point and ride from there, eliminating the steep climb.
Mileage: 18.5 miles. 12 miles if you drive to the top of the ridge.
Elevation: 4,560 ft. to 5,600 feet.
Water: At North Fork Campground and at streams along the ride. Be sure to filter or treat all water you take from mountain streams.

0.0 mile - From North Fork Campground, turn right onto Texas Hill Road. Ride past Onion Valley, the big meadow on your left. 0.5 miles - When the road splits, stay right on Forest Road 19, following the signs to Tunnel Mill Campground and Helester Point. Forest Road 19 goes downhill, following the East Fork of the North Fork of the American River. 1.5 miles - Ride past Tunnel Mill Campground, then begin the climb up to Texas Hill. 3.3 miles - At the top of the ridge, turn right, following the signs to Helester Point. At Forest Road 19, turn left. (See Ride #4.) 3.5 miles - A road takes off to the right and circles around Texas Hill for another ride option. Continue straight ahead. The road

Wooden bridge crossing

winds into Burnett Canyon, crosses the creek then winds back out the other side of the canyon and climbs up onto Sawtooth Ridge. The view gets spectacular as you ride along the edge of Sawtooth Ridge, with a 3,000 feet drop-off to the North Fork of the American River. The Foresthill Divide Area, Chapter 7, is located on the ridge to the south.

7.2 miles - The road splits and either way takes you to Helester Point. The best route is to go left, following the sign to the Mumford Bar Trail, marked *19/16/9*. 7.8 miles - A road to the left with a gate across it leads to Government Springs and Mumford Bar Trail. (Mumford Bar Trail is only for really adventurous riders. Those who are strong enough can actually ride down into the canyon 3,000 feet below to the American River, then climb back up the other side to Foresthill Divide. *Don't try the trail alone. Be sure to look at a topo map first.*) Continue straight ahead. 9.1 miles - When Road 19/16/9 ends, you must make a decision. Ride #3 continues on to the left. To finish Ride #2, turn right and follow the signs to North Fork Campground and Interstate 80. 11.2 miles - Back at the intersection with the road to Mumford Bar, continue straight ahead and follow your tracks back to the campground.

#3   Helester Point

Level of Difficulty: Strong intermediate or better. This ride is a longer version of Ride #2 and involves an additional 5 miles with a lot of short ups and downs.
Mileage: 24 miles out and back.
Elevation: 4,760 ft. to 6,410 ft.

0.0 mile - From North Fork Campground, follow the description for Ride #2 for the first 9.1 miles. Then turn left (west), following the signs to Helester Point. From here the road is easy to follow; just stay on the main road. This road goes down and up several times, following the

Sawtooth Ridge line out, then descends to an old lookout point, 2.6 miles farther on, ending with a magnificent view into the canyon below. When you have finished enjoying the view, follow your tracks back to the last intersection. 14.3 miles - Road 19/16/9 takes off to the right. Go straight ahead at this point. When you reach the intersection for the road to Mumford Bar, continue straight ahead and follow your tracks back to the campground.

#4   Big Valley Bluff

Level of Difficulty: Intermediate. The ride out is almost all uphill, so the return trip is fun and easy. Beginners may want to try this one by driving to the end of the pavement at the 3.3 mile point. From there it's a moderate 6.5 mile ride.
Mileage: 13 miles total.
Elevation: 4,760 ft. to 6,409 ft.

0.0 mile - From North Fork Campground follow Ride #2 for the first 3.3 miles. At 3.3 miles continue on out Forest Road 19, following the signs to Big Valley Bluff. Stay on the main road, passing several roads which lead off right and left. Continue to climb up on the ridge. 6.5 miles - Turn right at the sign to Big Valley Bluff. Forest Road 19 continues straight ahead. The road climbs 100 feet higher, then as you get out onto Big Valley Bluff you descend to a view point looking down into the steep North Fork of the American River Canyon, more than 3,000 feet below. When you have enjoyed the view, follow your tracks, climbing back up the bluff. From this point the ride is nearly all downhill to the campground!

#5   Onion Valley/Sailor Point Loop

Level of Difficulty: Intermediate; for those who enjoy a bit of adventure trying to find old abandoned roads to ride. The ride can be done in both directions.
Mileage: 9 miles.
Elevation: 4,560 ft. to 5,410 ft.

0.0 mile - From North Fork Campground, turn right on Texas Hill Road. 0.5 miles - At Onion Valley, turn left at the sign to Monument Creek. 0.6 miles - Turn left again and ride along the southeast side of Onion Valley which is one large meadow after another. 1.6 miles - Just before the top of the hill, look off to your left for an old road that is almost overgrown with brush. Ride out the old, narrow road that crosses a creek and climbs up through a rocky wash. (You may have to walk a

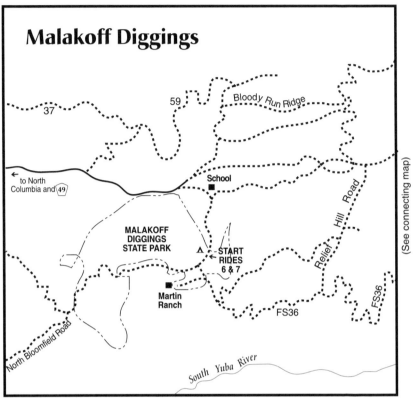

Malakoff Diggings

©1997 Fine Edge Productions

short section here.) Once you're on top, the road gets better and widens out. Stay on the main road which takes you past some homes. 3.1 miles - When the road ends at a large opening, turn left and you should see a green Forest Service Gate signed *Sailor Point Road*. Ride out Sailor Point Road which climbs at first, then goes downhill. 7.1 miles - Turn left on Texas Hill Road and enjoy the downhill back to the campground.

MALAKOFF DIGGINGS

Every trip to the Northern Gold Country should include a visit to Malakoff Diggings (or "Diggins") State Historic Park, on the western edge of Tahoe National Forest, to see the effect of large-scale hydraulic mining, which occurred in numerous areas throughout the Sierra

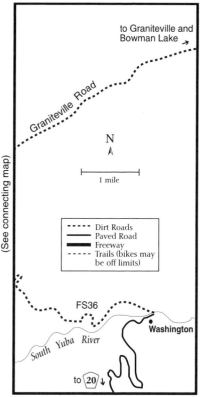

to Graniteville and
Bowman Lake

Graniteville Road

N

1 mile

(See connecting map)

Dirt Roads
Paved Road
Freeway
Trails (bikes may
be off limits)

FS36

Washington

South Yuba River

to 20

©1997 Fine Edge Productions

Nevada foothills. Within the park is the site of the largest hydraulic gold mine in the world (operated 1866-1884). Although the mining tore away nearly half a mountain, the destruction resulted in the creation of cliff walls similar to the sandstone spires and natural formations found in Utah. You can view the diggings by mountain bike from the roads. But to get a closer look you have to walk because all the hiking trails within the Park are closed to mountain bikes. The State Park is on the edge of the National Forest, so finding a place to ride is not a problem if you stay here.

To get to the park, take Interstate 80 to Auburn; go north on Highway 49 through Grass Valley and Nevada City. Twelve miles north of Nevada City, turn right on Tyler Foote Crossing Road and continue to the park.

Trailhead Location: State Park campground, T18N, R10E, Section 31.
Topo Maps: Pike, Washington, North Bloomfield, Alleghany, 7.5 min . Alleghany, 15 min.
Campgrounds: A small campground is located at the State Park, with a small lake nearby for swimming and fishing.
Water: Within the campground and at several locations throughout the park.
Seasons: Malakoff Diggings State Park is open year-round. Elevation levels range from 2,000 feet to over 4,000 feet, so you can try winter riding here except during low-elevation snowstorms.
Nearest Services: Small stores are located along Highway 49, but major supplies, gas and bike parts are available in Nevada City or Grass Valley.

The Malakoff School

#6   Relief Hill Loop

The Relief Hill Loop ride takes you out of the State Park into the National Forest with an option of riding farther out to the historic town of Washington where you can see several old restored buildings.

Level of Difficulty: Intermediate, with a gradual but steady climb in the beginning and a steep fast downhill. All of the road surfaces are good dirt with a minimal amount of rocks. (The optional ride to Washington is for advanced riders only.)
Mileage: 13 miles; 29 miles if you detour out to the town of Washington and back before completing the loop.
Elevation: 3,300 ft. to 4,600 ft. If you do the optional ride out to Washington, the road goes down into the canyon to 2,600 ft. to the South Yuba River.

0.0. mile - From the campground turn left on the main road (Bloomfield), which climbs back up to the ridge. 0.8 mile - When the road splits just before the grammar school, stay right and ride past the school. The road through here is gravel, dirt, with oiled sections. 4.0 miles - Continue straight ahead at the four-way intersection, staying on the gravel road. 5.8 miles - Turn right on the dirt road signed *Snowtent Rd./Relief Hill.* Your uphill is over and now it is time to start back down into the canyon. 6.9 miles - A road takes off to the left. Continue on down the hill following the signs to Relief Hill. 8.4 miles - The road to the left goes to the town of Washington, 8 miles farther, another historic town you might want to visit by bike. To finish the loop, stay to the right following the signs to North Bloomfield. Soon you will pass by some old cabins and new homes. Continue on. 11.2 miles - When the road ends, turn right. 12 miles - You are back in the Park in the historic town of North Bloomfield. Turn right, ride past the museum, and stay on this road back to the campground.

#7   Martin Ranch

Level of Difficulty: Easy; suitable for all levels of mountain bikers. This short, easy ride takes you through the State Park, then on to a fire road to the old Martin Ranch.
Mileage: 3 miles out and back.
Elevation: 3,200 ft. to 3,400 ft.

0.0 mile - From the campground, turn right and ride back down to the old town of North Bloomfield. 0.5 miles - Turn left on Relief Road, also marked Forest Road 36. The hiking trail to Martin Ranch takes off on your left. Bikes are not allowed on the trails so continue a short distance on Relief Road to the fire road. 1.0 miles - Look off to your right and you should see the fire road closed off by a wood pole gate. Go around the gate and ride out the fire road to the Martin Ranch. 1.5 miles - Explore the old Martin Ranch site, then return to the campground by retracing your tracks.

WASHINGTON AREA

Deep in a forested canyon, alongside the South Yuba River, is the quaint little town of Washington (population about 200). Today a few historic old buildings and some of the charm remain from what was once a bustling gold mining area before the turn of the century.

A group of prospectors from Indiana first struck it rich here in 1849, and the settlement was known briefly as Indiana Camp. By 1850, over a thousand men lived and worked here, finding the South Yuba

River and the creeks that feed it rich with gold. Over the next few years the area's population swelled to over 4,000 people, and dozens of buildings appeared.

The centerpiece of Washington is the beautiful old Washington Hotel. Originally built in 1850, the structure you see today was the third building bearing that name, being erected immediately after the second one burned to the ground in 1896. Having recently obtained the designation "historic" for the Washington Hotel, current owner Henry deCorte is finishing an extensive renovation. There are 16 rooms available, and Room 9 is where the famous lawman Wyatt Earp once stayed! If you would like to reserve a room, call (916) 265-4364.

For several years, this section of the South Yuba River has been a favorite with whitewater kayakers during periods of spring runoff; others have found the surrounding National Forest lands to provide a wealth of outdoor recreational opportunities. Recently, Washington has also become a favorite starting point for mountain bikers, especially those who enjoy climbing.

To get to Washington from Interstate 80, take Highway 20 toward Nevada City. After 14 miles, turn right onto Washington Road.

The historic Washington Hotel

Follow this winding, downhill road for 5.1 miles to the town of Washington.

Trailhead Location: All rides start from the town of Washington, T17N, R10E, Section 12.

Topo Maps: Washington, Alleghany, Blue Canyon, Graniteville 7.5 min.

Campgrounds: In the town of Washington, there are two private campgrounds–River Rest and Pineaire–along the river.

Water: Available within the campgrounds and from streams/rivers along some sections of the rides. Be sure to treat or filter all water you take from streams or lakes.

Seasons: Most of the year except for the dead of winter, presuming you can get to Washington and there has not recently been a low-elevation snowstorm or heavy rain.

Nearest Services: Meals and lodging are available at the Washington Hotel. Groceries, beverages, and snacks may be obtained at the Washington General Store or at the campgrounds. Gas, bike parts, and accessories may be found in Nevada City or Grass Valley.

#8   Gaston Road Climb

This relentless ascent up Gaston Ridge from Washington to Graniteville Road has become very popular. Once you reach Graniteville Road, consider turning left and descending to the village of Graniteville (no services, but an interesting place), or turning right for more climbing, followed by a descent to Bowman Lake.

Level of Difficulty: Not difficult from a technical perspective, but tough because of the endurance required to make the climb. This ride is for strong intermediates, and for advanced riders if your route includes a run over to Graniteville.
Mileage: 21.5 miles up to Graniteville Road and back. The ride to Graniteville adds a little over 4 miles out and back on a rougher road; riding to Bowman Lake adds a bit over 8 miles.
Elevation: 2,610 ft. to 5, 540 ft.

0.0 mile - Ride east out of Washington, across the South Yuba River. 0.5 mile - Turn left. A small sign shows you are heading toward Bowman Lake. 0.8 mile - You reach a "Y" with a sign indicating *Graniteville 12 miles* and *Bowman Lake 14 miles.* (The left fork, Forest Service Road 36, heads off to Relief Hill Road–see rides #6 and #10.) Bear right at the "Y" onto Gaston Road, also called Gaston Grade Road, and begin a 10-

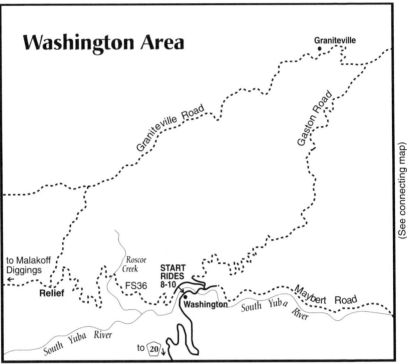

Washington Area

Graniteville

Graniteville Road

Gaston Road

(See connecting map)

to Malakoff
Diggings
←

*Roscoe
Creek*

START
RIDES
8-10

Relief

FS36

Washington *South Yuba River*

Maybert Road

South Yuba River

to 20

©1997 Fine Edge Productions

mile climb with an elevation gain of nearly 3,000 feet. Just stay on the main road, which is wide and well maintained.

10.8 miles - At the "T," you have reached Graniteville Road. For an out-and-back ride of 21.5 miles, turn around here and head back to Washington. The road is good, so the return trip is remarkably quick.

If you would like to extend the ride, you have two choices. A left turn and 2 miles, with a 600-foot descent, takes you to Graniteville, a very small village with only 20 buildings or so and no services. A right turn at the "T" takes you over a little pass (600 feet additional elevation gain) and then down to Bowman Lake. This area is very beautiful, and Bowman Lake is one of the larger lakes in Tahoe National Forest.

#9   South Yuba River

Level of Difficulty: This is a delightful, scenic beginner ride following the South Yuba River. It is all on good road (mostly dirt) and involves less than 600 feet of climbing.
Mileage: 7 miles out and back.
Elevation: 2,610 ft. to 3,180 ft.

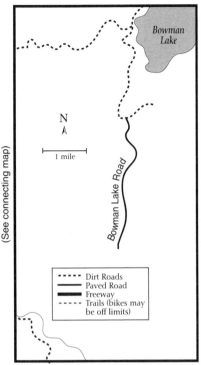

Bowman
Lake

N
⋀

├──── 1 mile ────┤

Bowman Lake Road

(See connecting map)

····· Dirt Roads
──── Paved Road
━━━━ Freeway
- - - - Trails (bikes may
be off limits)

©1997 Fine Edge Productions

0.0 mile - Follow Ride #8 for 0.5 mile. Then, don't turn left, but continue straight ahead, following the South Yuba River on Maybert Road. 0.7 mile - The paved road turns to dirt. 1.3 miles - You pass Keleher Picnic Ground. Stop here for restrooms, river access, photos, or whatever. 3.1 miles - A sign indicates Holbrook Flat. 3.5 miles - You reach a bridge crossing the river. This is the end of the county road and a good place to take a rest and check out the river. From here you turn around and head back to Washington for a total of 7.0 miles. Stronger riders can consider following the road on past the bridge for another few miles to get to the Golden Quartz Campground, an area of primitive campsites along the river.

#10   Roscoe Creek Climb

Following a well-used jeep trail, this out-and-back ride to Roscoe Creek on Forest Service Road 36 has a nice mixture of uphills and downhills and occasional flat sections, all with great scenery.

It is easy to lengthen the ride if you want more mileage. Road 36 is the one mentioned in Ride #6—coming from Washington, you can take it west all the way to Malakoff Diggings via the Relief Hill Loop for a long, tough ride of 29 miles!

Level of Difficulty: Intermediate or better.
Mileage: 9.2 miles out and back.
Elevation: 2,610 ft. to 3,420 ft.

0.0 mile - Follow Ride #8 for 0.8 mile, then bear left at the fork onto Forest Service Road 36. 1.1 miles - Ride past the entrance to Pineaire Campground, and 0.1 mile later, the road turns to dirt. 2.4 miles - You cross the bridge over Poorman Creek. The elevation here is essentially the same as when you started, but the next couple of miles are almost all climbing. (Beginners may elect to turn around here for an out-and-back ride of 4.8 miles.)

3.3 miles - You pass a road headed downhill to the left (green pole gate). Continue straight, mostly climbing. At 4.6 miles you reach Roscoe Creek (signed), a place to pause and decide whether or not to keep climbing. Turning here will give you a very scenic ride of 9.2 miles. If you continue straight ahead for another 3.5 miles, you will reach "Relief," the southeast corner of the Relief Hill Loop.

CHAPTER 3

🚲

Bowman Lake Area

The Bowman Lake area is located 40 miles east of Auburn, north of Interstate 80, at elevations between 5,500 and 7,500 feet. The fun about riding here is that there are so many lakes so close together that you can ride to several in one day! This is a wonderful spot to visit if you enjoy canoeing, swimming and fishing in addition to mountain biking. Trails and roads are very well marked. You will be riding in and out of private and public lands, so always remember to respect the private property signs.

There are three ways to get here. One is to drive east on Interstate 80 and take the Highway 20 off-ramp (1 mile east of the Yuba Gap turnoff), following the signs toward Nevada City. Go west on Highway 20 for 3.5 miles to Bowman Lake Road (Forest Road 18). Follow the signs along the Bowman Lake Road to the trailhead or campground of your choice. Be aware that most of the side roads are dirt, and the main road turns to dirt just before reaching Bowman Lake, 13 miles out. The road along the north shore of Bowman Lake is quite narrow in spots and definitely more fun on a bike than in a car!

Another approach is to take Highway 49 north to Tyler Foote Crossing Road. Go east past North Columbia and Malakoff Diggings to the town of Graniteville. From Graniteville continue east on a county road following the signs to Bowman Lake (see map on next page).

To access the northern part of this area, go 17 miles north of Truckee on Highway 89, turn left (west) on Forest Road 07 and drive 16 miles to Jackson Meadow Reservoir. Forest Road 07 is paved all the way to the reservoir but turns to dirt just past the campgrounds.

Campgrounds: There are plenty of undeveloped U.S. Forest Service campgrounds here. They have outhouses, but may not have tables or

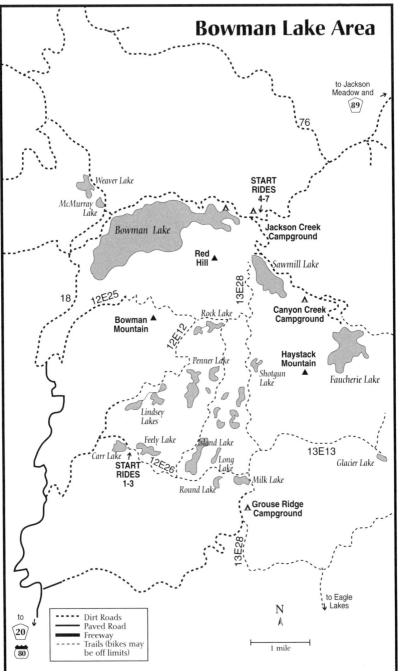

Bowman Lake Area

to Jackson
Meadow and
89

76

Weaver Lake

McMurray
Lake

Bowman Lake

**START
RIDES
4-7**

**Jackson Creek
Campground**

Red
Hill

Sawmill Lake

13E28

18   12E25

**Bowman
Mountain**

Rock Lake

**Canyon Creek
Campground**

12E12

Penner Lake

**Haystack
Mountain**

Shotgun
Lake

Faucherie Lake

Lindsey
Lakes

Feely Lake

Island Lake

Carr Lake

**START
RIDES
1-3**

12E26

Long
Lake

13E13

Glacier Lake

Milk Lake

Round Lake

**Grouse Ridge
Campground**

13E28

N

to Eagle
Lakes

to
20

80

- - - - Dirt Roads
———— Paved Road
▬▬▬▬ Freeway
- - - Trails (bikes may
be off limits)

1 mile

©1997 Fine Edge Productions

water systems. No fee is charged at undeveloped campgrounds. The better camping facilities, complete with water and tables, are located at Jackson Meadows Reservoir, Grouse Ridge and Lake Spaulding. There is public land available for primitive camping, but be aware that there is also a great deal of private property that is posted *No Camping - No Trespassing*. Also, in certain parts of this area camping is allowed only within the campgrounds. (Closed areas are marked on the Tahoe National Forest Map.)

Seasons: Late May through October.

Nearest Services: Take everything you need with you (food, ice, gas), since there are no services once you leave Interstate 80 or Highway 89. Nearest bike shops are in Truckee or Nevada City/Grass Valley.

CARR LAKE TRAILHEAD

Trailhead Location: Carr Lake Trailhead, T18N, R12E, Section 28. To get to Carr Lake, drive 8.5 miles out Forest Road 18 and turn right on Forest Road 17. Follow the signs to Carr and Feely Lakes, 3 miles farther. There is a small primitive campground located along the shore of Carr Lake. Forest Road 17 is dirt, so if you have a car rather than a truck, you may choose to start cycling from Forest Road 18, which will lengthen all of the following rides by 6 miles (3 miles each way). These rides can also be done from the campground at Grouse Ridge. Take the Grouse Ridge Trail northeast out of the campground toward Milk Lake. Follow the directions for the rides below from the trail intersection at the 2.2 mile point.

Topo Maps: English Mountain and Graniteville, 7.5 min., or Emigrant Gap, 15 min.

Water: There are lakes and streams everywhere. Be sure to filter or treat all drinking water.

#1   Shotgun Lake

Level of Difficulty: Beginner to intermediate trail riding. This is a short fun ride. Although most of this route is singletrack, many trails are wide old jeep roads. Some riders may have to get off and push through short uphill sections. If you want a more challenging ride, continue past Shotgun Lake, following directions for Ride #2.

Mileage: 10 miles out and back.

Elevation: 6,600 ft. to 7,100 ft.

Feely Lake and the Round Lake trailhead

0.0 mile - From Carr Lake, turn left on the road just before the out-houses in the campground. Ride uphill to Feely Lake. 0.1 mile - You arrive at Feely Lake and the Round Lake Trailhead (12E26) for Island Lake, Milk Lake and Grouse Ridge Campground. Continue on the Round Lake Trail. 1.0 mile - After you pass a pond and a small lake, the trail forks. The left fork is called Crooked Lake Trail, 12E11. (This is the trail you will return on if you choose to do the Island Lake Loop). Stay to the right, ride up over the ridge and you will arrive at Island Lake. 1.5 miles - Stay on the main trail. (The fork that leads to the right goes to Round Lake.) 1.6 miles - Turn right on the main trail. 1.7 miles - Turn left, following the sign to Milk Lake. 2.2 miles - At the top of a small hill you reach another intersection. The trail straight ahead goes to Grouse Ridge Campground. Off to the right is Milk Lake. Take the Grouse Ridge Trail to the left, following the sign to Glacier Lake and Sawmill Lake.

3.0 miles - At another intersection, stay to the left on the Grouse Ridge Trail. (The road to the right goes to Glacier Lake Trail, 13E13.) 4.3 miles - You reach Middle Lake, which is on its way to becoming Middle Meadow. Continue on the main trail. 4.7 miles - You reach a large meadow and a new section of trail that keeps you up on the rocks and out of the wet meadow. 5.0 miles - You arrive at Shotgun Lake, which is also almost a meadow. From here you can continue on 0.8 mile farther to the edge of the canyon. When you are ready, follow your tracks back to Carr Lake.

#2 Island Lake Loop

Level of Difficulty: Advanced. Don't be fooled by the low mileage of this ride. It gets rough after you leave Shotgun Lake. Warning! Do not continue if you think the ride to Shotgun is tough, go back the way you came. This section of trail is very rocky and very technical, but also very scenic and enjoyable for those in the right frame of mind who don't mind walking occasionally. Great for people who enjoy trials riding or like to work on bike handling skills.
Mileage: 11 miles.
Elevation: 6,600 ft. to 7,100 ft. You will lose and gain 500 feet several times throughout this ride.

0.0 mile - From Carr Lake, follow the directions for Ride #1 to Shotgun Lake. Continue north on the main trail. 5.8 miles - At the edge of the canyon turn left on the trail signed *Bull Pen Trail 12E12 - Rock Lake 1 mile.* Straight ahead the Grouse Ridge Trail descends 1 mile to Sawmill Lake. You can ride down to Sawmill Lake for a longer ride, but you will probably have to push your way back up to this intersection. *Warning! On the maps this trail looks like it easily connects to the road on the other side of Sawmill Lake, but if there is a lot of water flowing out of Sawmill Lake the creek crossing is quite dangerous.* You may have to go downstream quite a distance before finding a safe place to cross.

Walk and ride your bike up 380 feet to the top of the ridge. 6.8 miles - At the top, stay left and follow the signs to Penner Lake. (Rock Lake is off to the right. Another option here is to ride out to Lindsey Lake and follow the dirt road back to your car.) After a short downhill, most people will have to walk up some of the next section, which climbs another 400 feet before dropping down to Penner Lake. 7.5 miles - Stay on the trail that follows along the east shore of Penner Lake. *Be careful as you climb and descend through the next rocky sections.* You may want to lower your seat and let some air out of your tires, but don't let too much air out because these sharp rocks could easily puncture a tire. 8.6 miles - You will begin to pass Crooked Lakes off to the left (east). 9.0 miles - Begin the final rocky downhill to Island Lake. The trail continues along the west shore. 9.5 miles - You are back at the intersection of trail 12E26 to Grouse Ridge. Turn right to return to Carr Lake. 10.4 miles - Feely Lake. Continue on to the spillway and back to your car.

#3   Glacier Lake

Level of Difficulty: Intermediate or better riders that have trail riding experience.
Mileage: 12 miles out and back.
Elevation: 6,600 ft. to 7,600 ft.

0.0 mile - From Carr Lake, follow Ride #1 the first 3 miles. 3.0 miles -Go right on Trail 13E13 following the signs to Glacier Lake. This trail continues on another 3 miles and climbs about 500 feet to the lake. There are places you may have to push your bike. 6.0 miles - Enjoy the lake, which is surrounded by the Black Buttes. When you are ready, follow your tracks or ride back to the intersection and do Ride #2.

JACKSON CREEK CAMPGROUND TRAILHEAD

Jackson Creek Campground is located just east of Bowman Lake. Take Interstate 80 to Highway 20 and turn right on Bowman Lakes Road. Continue on along the north shore of Bowman Lake (the road turns to dirt just before the lake). Jackson Creek Campground is located just past the lake. You can also reach this area from the northeast by taking Highway 89, turning west on Forest Road 07 and continuing to Jackson Meadow Reservoir. After you pass the Jackson Meadow Campground area the road turns to dirt. Continue southwest 3.7 miles to Jackson Creek Campground. If you would rather not drive your car on dirt roads, camp at Jackson Meadows Reservoir and do the rides from there. This will add an additional 8 miles to each of the following routes (4 miles each way).

Trailhead Location: All rides in this section begin at Jackson Creek Campground, T18N, R12E, Section 2.
Topo Maps: English Mountain 7.5 min., or Emigrant Gap 15 min.
Campgrounds: USFS campgrounds are located at Jackson Meadows Reservoir, Bowman Lake, Canyon Creek and also at Jackson Creek, where the rides begin.
Water: These campgrounds do not have water systems, with the exception of those at Jackson Meadows Reservoir. Water is not a problem in summer because the lakes are all controlled by utility companies, and the flow is usually good year-round. Be sure to filter or treat all water from mountain streams.

#4   Faucherie Lake

Level of Difficulty: Easy beginner ride, scenic and enjoyable for all riders. This is a fun ride on good dirt road with rocky sections. Watch your speed on the way back down—the rough sections may catch you by surprise.
Mileage: 8 miles out and back.
Elevation: Gradual 500-foot gain, 5,600 ft. to 6,123 ft.

0.0 mile - From Jackson Creek Campground, ride south on Faucherie Road. 1.2 miles - Continue straight at the intersection. The road to the right goes to Sawmill Lake, which you could go explore now or on your way back. (Ride out to the spillway, and if you hit it at a time when there is water spilling over the top you will be treated to a series of spectacular water falls!) 2.0 miles - A spur road to the left goes over to a waterfall on Canyon Creek. If you can hear the falls, then it is probably worth riding over to take a look. Continue straight ahead on the main road. 2.5 miles - Continue on past Canyon Creek Campground, another nice place to camp. 3.8 miles - You arrive at Faucherie Lake, clear blue and surrounded by barren, granite peaks. A quiet place to spend the day fishing, swimming and picnicking, this also looks like a nice lake for canoeing. Be sure to ride across the dam to see if water is going over the spillway. Across the spillway you should be able to see a rocky road, which is the road you take to Canyon Creek (Ride #5). When you are through exploring and swimming, follow your tracks back to your car.

#5   Canyon Creek

Level of Difficulty: Intermediate or better. Even though this is a very low mileage trip, it is not for beginners. It is good for those who enjoy mountain biking as an adventure, and don't mind pushing their bikes a bit to get to those hidden spots that very few people visit. It has fun trials riding sections, and Upper Canyon Creek also looks like a great place to try your luck at fishing.
Mileage: 9 miles out and back.
Elevation: 5,600 ft. to 6,400 ft.

0.0 mile - From Jackson Creek Campground, follow Ride #4 for the first 2.5 miles. 2.5 miles - Turn left on the road just across from Canyon Creek Campground. Stay to the right. This is the back way to the Faucherie Lake spillway. The road is short but fun if you enjoy rocky, trials-type riding. 3.5 miles - When you reach the spillway, there may

Wet and wild creek crossing

be a lot of water flowing out of the lake and the road might be under water for a short distance. Walk along the left shore and you should be able to get around the flooded section and get back to the road. 3.7 miles - You ride along the shores of Faucherie Lake, heading back to the inlet of Canyon Creek.

As you leave the lake and begin to follow the creek, the road turns into more of a trail and becomes even rockier in spots. Some may choose to continue on foot; others will find this section a challenge. 4.4 miles - The trail reaches a large bend in the creek with cascading rapids and waterfalls. If you continue from here you will have to portage your bike around a cliff to get to Weil Lake about 0.5 mile farther upstream. (Walking is recommended from this point.) When you have finished exploring, follow your tracks back to camp.

#6   Bowman, Weaver and McMurray Lakes

Level of Difficulty: Basically a beginner ride with one good climb. Beginners may choose to ride to the end of Bowman Lake and back instead.
Mileage: Weaver Lake and back, 9 miles. Bowman Lake spillway and back, 6 miles.
Elevation: 5,623 ft. to 5,850 ft.

0.0 mile - From Jackson Creek Campground ride west on the Bowman Lakes Road. 0.7 mile - You reach the upper end of Bowman Lake and the Bowman Lake Campground. For the next 2+ miles, the road follows the shoreline of Bowman Lake. Watch for traffic—the road is quite narrow! 2.7 miles - Turn right on the dirt road that immediately starts to climb. There should be a sign here that reads *McMurray Lake 1 mile - Weaver Lake 2 miles*. This road climbs steeply to the top of a ridge and McMurray Lake. From here the road goes gradually downhill. 4.5 miles - Weaver Lake, elevation 5,688 ft. Prepare for a fun downhill back to Bowman Lake and follow your tracks to the campground.

Option from Weaver Lake: The road continues past Weaver Lake and from the map it looks like you could make a long loop around Pinole Ridge on Forest Road 41, then turn right on Forest Road 76, which takes you back to the Bowman Lakes Road and Jackson Creek Campground. If you choose this route you will be riding in and out of private land. The total mileage for the loop is about 19 miles. Carry a topo map and a National Forest Map.

#7   Meadow Lake

Level of Difficulty: Intermediate or better. You will gain 2,000 feet in elevation; however, the road surface is all dirt and not too technical.
Mileage: 19.5 miles out and back.
Elevation: 5,623 ft. to 7,600 ft.
Topo Maps: 7.5 min. English Mountain and Webber Peak, or 15 min. Emigrant Gap and Donner Pass.

0.0 mile - From Jackson Creek Campground go east following the signs to Jackson Meadows Reservoir. The road climbs about 600 feet in the next two miles, travelling mainly through private land. Off to your right you will see English Mountain Ranch, a large meadow with English Mountain in the background. 2.8 miles - Turn right on road 19N11, following the signs to Catfish Lake and Meadow Lake. 3.8 miles - The main road continues past Catfish Lake, which is surrounded by private land. From here it goes downhill about a mile before it begins to climb, gradually at first, then rather steeply in spots back up to over 7,600 feet. 8.8 miles - The climbing is over and you get to enjoy a downhill to Meadow Lake. 9.7 miles - At the intersection turn left to ride along the shore of Meadow Lake. When you are ready to return, follow your tracks. There are a couple of uphills on the way back to Jackson Creek Campground, but most of the work is over and the return ride is primarily a downhill run.

EAGLE MOUNTAIN CROSS COUNTRY AND MOUNTAIN BIKING PARK

Location: On Interstate 80, 38 miles east of Auburn (74 miles east of Sacramento), take the Yuba Gap off-ramp. Turn right and follow the signs for "Eagle Mountain Nordic" about 1 mile farther to Eagle Mountain. Park in the parking lot and go into the lodge to purchase a trail pass.

Campgrounds: The people at Eagle Mountain recommend the campground at Lake Spaulding, located just north of Interstate 80. There are several others located nearby on both sides of the freeway.

Seasons: Eagle Mountain Cross Country and Mountain Biking Park is open from late May to the middle of October.

Nearest Services: Eagle Mountain has a repair shop, and the people there should be able to help you with anything you need for your bike. They also have a good supply of cycling accessories—shorts, shirts, sunglasses, sunscreen, etc.—and a snack bar to take care of your pre- and post-ride food needs. Gas stations and grocery stores are located in Cisco Grove east on Interstate 80.

Details: Call (916) 389-2254 for more information, an events calendar, and for current fee information. The people at Eagle Mountain organize races (including some on snow) and lead around-the-park bike tours, bike handling skills classes, white water raft trips and rock climbing excursions. Rental bikes are available at the lodge.

A cross-country ski center in winter, Eagle Mountain uses its trail system for a mountain bike park in summer. The bike park is located on 1,100 acres of private land between 5,800 ft. and 6,140 ft. in elevation. Eagle Mountain advertises 120 km. of maintained mountain bike trails.

Eagle Mountain and other winter recreation areas are experimenting with the idea of promoting summer recreation to develop into year-round resorts. The nice thing about this is that you can find a place to ride without having to spend too much time searching. Also, it is a great place to go if you have a group with a variety of riding skill levels. The trails and the trail map are clearly labeled according to the degree of difficulty, so beginners can ride the easy loops while the better riders try the more advanced trails. Afterwards you can meet at the lodge for lunch or snacks.

CHAPTER 4

🚲

Cisco Grove Area

INDIAN SPRINGS TRAILHEAD

The rides in this chapter are located along Interstate 80, 45 miles east of Auburn at 5,400 to 7,400 feet near the town of Cisco Grove. Along this section, Interstate 80 travels through a canyon following the South Fork of the Yuba River. Campgrounds are located close to the river so you can bike all day then return to your campsite in the afternoon to swim and fish. The choice of rides in this area includes dirt logging roads, singletrack trails through the granite plateau of the Lakes Basin Area, and the challenging hill climb up to Signal Peak.

Take the Eagle Lakes turnoff about 2 miles west of Cisco Grove. Go northwest about a half mile to Indian Springs Campground. Find a campsite here, or continue on to the trailhead. To get to Indian Springs trailhead, turn right on the dirt road that takes off just past Indian Springs Campground (sign reads *Indian Springs Trailhead*). After a 0.2-mile drive down a dirt road, you arrive at the trailhead and parking area, which has a bulletin board and restrooms. If there is a map posted, be sure to stop and take a look. There is private land scattered throughout this area, and if there is heavy logging traffic a warning will be posted here.

Trailhead Location: Indian Springs Trailhead, T17N, R12E, Section 24.
Topo Maps: Cisco Grove 7.5 min., or Emigrant Gap 15 min.
Campgrounds: U.S. Forest Service campgrounds are located at Indian Springs and Big Bend, and there is a PG&E campground at Lake Spaulding. All of these are nice campgrounds with access to the South Fork of the Yuba River or the shore of Lake Spaulding. Unfortunately they are also near Interstate 80. The noise settles down at night, but this freeway is busy all the time.

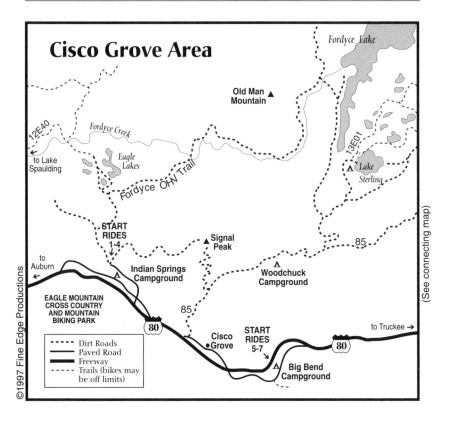

Cisco Grove Area

Fordyce Lake

Old Man ▲
Mountain

12E40

Fordyce Creek

to Lake
Spaulding

Eagle
Lakes

Fordyce OHV Trail

13E01

▲ Lake
Sterling

START
RIDES
1-4

Signal
▲ Peak

85

to
Auburn

Indian Springs
Campground

▲
Woodchuck
Campground

EAGLE MOUNTAIN
CROSS COUNTRY
AND MOUNTAIN
BIKING PARK

85

80

to Truckee →

Cisco
●Grove

START
RIDES
5-7

80

· · · · · Dirt Roads
——— Paved Road
▬▬▬ Freeway
- - - - Trails (bikes may
be off limits)

▲
Big Bend
Campground

(See connecting map)

©1997 Fine Edge Productions

Seasons: Mid-June through October.

Nearest Services: Grocery stores and gas stations are located 2 miles east on Interstate 80 in Cisco Grove. A U.S. Forest Service Ranger Station and information center is located in Big Bend, just east of Cisco Grove. Nearest bike shops would be in Auburn or at Eagle Mountain to the west, or in Truckee to the east.

#1   Eagle Lakes/Fordyce Bridge

Level of Difficulty: Short, fun and challenging intermediate level ride. It's great for those who like to ride the rocks, or want to learn how to ride them. Eagle Lakes vary in size; most of them partially covered with lilies. If you enjoy swimming, ride on to Fordyce Creek where you will find clear, cold water.

Mileage: 6 miles out and back to Eagle Lakes. Fordyce Bridge is 8 miles out and back.

Elevation: 5,400 ft. to 5,500 ft. This ride is nearly flat if you look on a topo map! But in truth you will gain and lose 100 feet in elevation many times over.

Water: Treated water is available from the campground at Indian Springs. If you

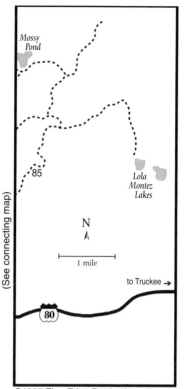

Mossy Pond

85

Lola Montez Lakes

N
⋏

1 mile

to Truckee →

80

(See connecting map)

©1997 Fine Edge Productions

need water out on the trail, take it from Fordyce Creek rather than from Eagle Lakes. Be sure to filter or treat all water.

0.0 mile - Ride out the Eagle Lakes jeep road which follows along the power line a short distance and then descends to the west. 0.9 mile - Turn right at the intersection following the sign to Eagle Lakes and Grouse Ridge Trail. (The road to the left goes into private land at Pierce Meadows.) 2.0 miles - The road turns into a rocky, washed-out area where jeeps have developed some detours around the worst spots. If you take the detours this whole section is rideable. 2.4 miles - Stay left on the main road, following the sign to Eagle Lakes and Grouse Ridge. (The road to the right goes to Fordyce OHV and Meadow Lake.) At 2.6 miles, stay right following the OHV arrow, then take the next road to the left about 0.1 mile farther. (If you turn right here, the road takes you directly to one of the Eagle Lakes, but the trail ends there and you have to bushwhack your way around the west shore to get back to the road).

3.0 miles - The road leads you between several of the Eagle Lakes. There are side trails taking off all along this next stretch if you would like to take a closer look. 3.3 miles - The road ends at a turnaround. Look north toward the rocks for the trail that leads to Fordyce Bridge. You will have to portage your bike a bit through the next section, so some people may choose to turn around here. 3.7 miles - The bridge over Fordyce Creek. There are nice spots to picnic and swim both upstream and downstream from the bridge. If you choose to swim, be careful! The water runs swiftly at different times of the summer. It is controlled by a utility company, and even late in August the creek may be quite full. Take a good look at the size of the bridge; at times this creek must be a major river!

On the far side of the bridge is a sign for Spaulding Trail, Beyers

Lake Trail and Grouse Ridge Campground. When you are through exploring, follow your tracks back.

Options: You could ride out the trail to Lake Spaulding (see Ride #2) or continue on the Beyers Lake Trail. However, the Beyers Lake Trail is not recommended for mountain bikes! On the map it looks quite tempting, but we pushed our bikes up the ridge (gaining over 800 feet) before we gave up, only to find we had to push our bikes on some of the downhill!

#2 Lake Spaulding

Level of Difficulty: Strong intermediate.
Mileage: 14 miles out and back.
Water: Plenty of water is available on this ride. Be sure to filter or treat all stream water before you drink it.

0.0 miles - From the Indian Springs Trailhead, follow Ride #1 for the first 3.7 miles. 3.7 miles - Ride across the Fordyce Bridge, and turn left following the sign to the Spaulding Trail. 4.0 miles - Go left at the sign that reads *Spaulding Lake Trail 12E40–Spaulding Lake 2 miles–Bowman Lake Road 4 miles.* From here the trail continues to follow Fordyce Creek downstream. Most of it is rideable, but you will have to carry your bike around a few spots. The peak to the south is Brady Mountain. 5.8 miles - The trail begins to follow along the north shore of Spaulding Lake, leading toward the powerhouse. 7.0 miles - Spend some time enjoying Spaulding Lake and then follow your tracks back. (If you continue on from here the trail becomes a road, and you can ride it to Bowman Lake Road and tie into the rides described in Chapter 3 for the Carr Lake Trailhead.)

#3 Signal Peak Hill Climb

Level of Difficulty: Advanced ride for those who enjoy the challenge of a rocky hill climb.
Mileage: 8 miles out and back.
Elevation: 5,500 ft. to 7,841 ft.

0.0 mile - The jeep road you are looking for takes off to the right just before the information sign and restroom at the OHV Trailhead. The road is signed: *Signal Peak Jeep Trail.* Another sign says that the road is maintained by a 4-wheel drive club. This ride is easy to follow, just stay on the main 4-wheel drive road that continues to climb to the top of the ridge. The road climbs 1,000 feet quickly within the first 1.5

miles. Then, as it turns north the climb continues, but at a more gradual incline. 3.4 miles - When the road turns east again, prepare yourself for the final 800 ft. of climbing to the top. Once on top enjoy the view down into the South Yuba River Canyon, rest and then prepare for a rapid descent down the mountain! Don't forget the rough sections.

#4 Fordyce OHV Trail to Meadow Lake

Level of Difficulty: Advanced riders who know how to use a map and compass.
Mileage: 20 miles out and back.
Elevation: 5,500 ft. to 7,300 ft.
Warning! If you want to ride this route, check with the PG&E personnel at Spaulding Reservoir to see if the Fordyce Crossing is advisable. This trail is rideable and is a good route for mountain bikes as long as you can safely cross Fordyce Creek, approximately 2 miles out. You may have to stop there, even in late summer. The flow of Fordyce Creek is controlled by PG&E, and we were told stories of Toyota pickups being washed downstream as they tried to cross the creek in August.

0.0 mile - Start from the Indian Springs Trailhead and follow Ride #1 for the first 2.4 miles. At that point, turn right and follow the Fordyce OHV Trail and the sign that reads: *Meadow Lake 10 miles.*

From here, you are on your own. The road climbs 600 feet in the first 1.5 miles, then drops back down to the Fordyce Creek crossing. After Fordyce Creek, the road follows along the creek and gradually climbs over the next 5.5 miles. The last 3 miles are another 1,400 feet uphill to Meadow Lake (elev. 7,287 ft.). This is another out-and-back ride, but there are several options of longer loops if you are looking for a spot to do some bike camping. (See Chapter 3, Ride #6.)

LAKE STERLING/GLACIER BASIN

The rides listed in this section can be done from Big Bend Campground near Cisco Grove, or shorter loops can be ridden directly from Lake Sterling. Lake Sterling (6,887 ft.) is remote, although it is just 6.5 miles northeast of Interstate 80. The winding, mountain road to the lake turns to dirt just as it leaves Cisco Grove. If you have a new car or a car with low clearance, you should start the rides from Cisco Grove or from Big Bend Campground. Lake Sterling lies on the edge of National Forest property within the section of Forest that is still checkerboarded with private land. There is an abundance of logging roads to explore within this area, but please respect the private property signs.

Rocky challenge

Trailhead Locations: Rides start from Cisco Grove, T17N, R13E, Section 29, or from Lake Sterling, T17N, R13E, Section 10.

Topo Maps: Cisco Grove, Soda Springs and Webber Peak 7.5 min., or Donner Pass and Emigrant Gap 15 min.

Campgrounds: There is a small 6-site campground located on the shore of Lake Sterling—a quiet, remote place to camp! There is also a large Boy Scout Camp nearby, so Lake Sterling may not always be as quiet as it was when we visited. Woodchuck Campground is a small campground situated 3 miles northeast of Interstate 80. It may be a better choice if you find that the Boy Scout Camp is in session! Another campground close to this area is the Big Bend Campground located across the South Fork of the Yuba River behind the U.S. Forest Service Station in Big Bend.

Water: Treated water is available at the Big Bend Campground. Lake Sterling and Woodchuck Campgrounds do not have a water system. All water taken from streams and lakes needs to be boiled, filtered or treated before drinking.

Seasons: Mid-June through October.

Nearest Services: Food, gas stations and restaurants can be found in Big Bend and Cisco Grove. The closest bike shops are in Truckee (east) and in Auburn or at Eagle Mountain (west).

#5   Cisco Grove to Lake Sterling/Fordyce Lake

Level of Difficulty: Intermediate. There is quite a bit of climbing to Fordyce Lake, Lake Sterling and Lola Montez. The main road up is fairly smooth, but side roads to each of the lakes are rocky.

Mileage: 15 miles out and back for Fordyce Lake; 13 miles out and back for Lake Sterling; 22 miles out and back for Lola Montez.

Elevation: 5,700 ft. to 7,100 ft. (Fordyce Summit).

0.0 mile - From Cisco Grove, go west on Hampshire Rock Road (the main street in town). 0.2 mile - Just before the road ends at Thousand Trails Park, turn right on Rattlesnake Road (Forest Road 85). It turns to dirt and takes you along the edge of the Thousand Trails Park. The road begins to climb after it passes the park. You will ride up a couple of switchbacks, and then the road heads back into a small, steep box canyon on Rattlesnake Creek. 3.0 miles - Pass Woodchuck Campground and continue on the main road. 3.5 miles - On your right is a 4-H Summer Camp. Continue on the main road, which begins to wind its way up the ridge. 4.6 miles - You come to a junction with a sign: *Lake Sterling 2 miles - Fordyce Lake 3 miles - Lola Montez 6 miles.* (Forest Road 85 continues straight ahead 6 miles to Lola Montez Lake. This is an option for a longer ride.) To go to Lake Sterling or Fordyce Lake turn left. After one more hairpin turn and a little more climbing the road reaches Fordyce Summit (7,089 ft.). 5.3 miles - The road forks. Continue straight ahead to Fordyce Lake (2 miles) or turn right to Lake Sterling. Both options are explained as follows:

Fordyce Lake: Get ready for a rough, wild downhill! The road drops from 7,089 feet at the summit to lake level at 6,402 feet in less than two miles! Fordyce Lake is a large, long reservoir in a deep canyon. You can ride along the southeast edge of the lake until you reach the spillway. This is an out-and-back ride, so when you are ready, climb up out of the canyon to the summit and enjoy the downhill back to Cisco Grove.

Lake Sterling: You climb just a little bit more, to 7,200 feet, before descending to the lake. The campground is at the end of the road. There is also a trail to the left that leads to the spillway. It is rideable, but some may prefer to walk. From here you could continue on to Ride #6 or Ride #7. When you are ready, follow your tracks back to your car.

#6   Glacier Lakes Basin Loop

This ride is a short loop through a granite area with many small lakes and ponds–and it is entirely on singletrack! You can start from Lake Sterling, if you camped there, or from Cisco Grove or Woodchuck Campground following Ride #5.

Level of Difficulty: Intermediate to advanced with sections of technical singletrack. Everyone will walk in places.
Mileage: 3.5 miles, all trail riding, so allow 2-3 hours to make it enjoyable; 16.5 miles from Cisco Grove.
Elevation: 7,000 ft. to 7,200 ft.

0.0 mile - From the Lake Sterling Campground look around the west shore for a trail. There are several, and they all lead to the spillway. 0.2 mile - Ride carefully across the spillway. Although it is hard to tell, the trail splits on the other side. Go left up what looks like an old jeep trail with hiking switchbacks. 0.3 mile - You reach a sign: *Glacier Lakes Basin Trail 13E01 - Mossy Pond West - Mossy Pond East.* Go left, heading toward Mossy Pond West. 0.8 mile - The trail goes down a short, steep section to the first pond. After crossing a creek it travels past several other small ponds. Except for a few large log crossings and narrow brush areas, this section is quite rideable. 1.4 miles - The trails meet at another intersection signed *Mossy Pond 2 miles - Lake Sterling 2 miles.* To finish the short loop, go right here, heading back toward Lake Sterling. Follow the trail that winds up and down and around more ponds before descending to Lake Sterling. Continue back to the spillway and campground.

#7 Mossy Pond Loop

Level of Difficulty: Intermediate riders or adventurous beginners willing to walk a bit. It's not a very difficult ride except for the singletrack. For an easier route, ride out and back on the 4-wheel drive road to Mossy Pond. This way you can play at the slabs without having to do the singletrack.
Mileage: 9 miles; 22 miles starting from Cisco Grove.
Elevation: 6,988 ft. to 7,360 ft. (from Cisco Grove 5,700 ft. to 7,360 ft.).

0.0 mile - Follow Ride #6 for the first 1.4 miles. At the sign, go left to Mossy Pond. 2.2 miles - The trail ends at a 4-wheel drive road. From here you can take a detour to the left to two more ponds (this detour will add 0.3 miles to the total). To finish the loop, go right. 2.5 miles - The road goes down a steep, fun downhill. 2.8 miles - You arrive at the largest pond, Mossy Pond East. For a good view down into Fordyce Canyon, walk over to the granite rocks on the north end of the pond. To continue the loop, stay on the 4-wheel drive road that leaves the lake and heads east. 3.2 miles - The road turns into a hillside of granite slabs! The main route is well marked by "jeepers," 4-wheel drive traffic and there is plenty of room to play on the rocks. This is a great spot to come and play a while! Practice your bike handling skills on the smooth granite or try hopping around in the rockier sections. When you are through playing, get back on the main trail that climbs to the top of the slabs, then leaves the rocks. Next you will ride past a large meadow.

4.7 miles - Go right at the intersection. (The road to the left has a gate on it and enters private land.) You will ride past another meadow before the road begins a brief climb. 5.7 miles - In an uphill hairpin turn, take the road to the right. (For a longer loop continue straight ahead, then turn right when you reach Forest Road 85). 6.8 miles - Continue straight ahead at this intersection. (A right turn here takes you down a wild downhill to the east end of Lake Sterling. It is fun, but you then have to bushwhack your way around the lake to try to find a trail.) After a little more climbing the road turns and you are treated to a great view of Signal Peak to the east and Old Man Mountain to the northeast. Then the road begins to go downhill to the next intersection. 8.2 miles - Turn right and make the final descent back to Lake Sterling.

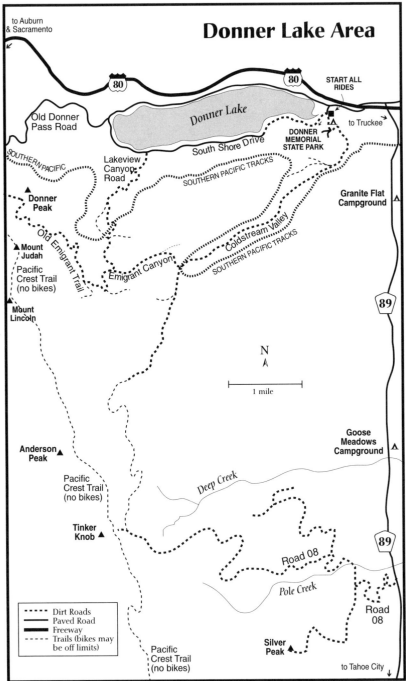

Donner Lake Area

to Auburn
& Sacramento

START ALL
RIDES

Old Donner
Pass Road

Donner Lake

to Truckee

DONNER
MEMORIAL
STATE PARK

South Shore Drive

SOUTHERN PACIFIC

Lakeview
Canyon
Road

SOUTHERN PACIFIC TRACKS

Granite Flat
Campground

Donner
Peak

Old Emigrant Trail

Coldstream Valley

Mount
Judah

Pacific
Crest Trail
(no bikes)

Emigrant Canyon

SOUTHERN PACIFIC TRACKS

Mount
Lincoln

N

1 mile

Anderson
Peak

Goose
Meadows
Campground

Pacific
Crest Trail
(no bikes)

Deep Creek

Tinker
Knob

Road 08

Pole Creek

Road
08

Dirt Roads
Paved Road
Freeway
Trails (bikes may
be off limits)

Pacific
Crest Trail
(no bikes)

Silver
Peak

Pacific
Crest Trail
(no bikes)

to Tahoe City

©1997 Fine Edge Productions

CHAPTER 5

🚲

Donner Lake Area

The Donner Summit area is rich in California history. Everywhere you ride, you will be reminded of the early pioneers who travelled through here on their journeys to the west. Monuments are dedicated to the tragic journey of the Donner Party, who tried to cross the Sierra during the winter of 1846-47, and to the amazing tunnel, dug by hand, through the mountains to complete the Central Pacific Railroad. If you enjoy history, be sure to visit the museum at the entrance to Donner Memorial State Park.

This is a wonderful place to visit in summer, but like the rest of the area along Interstate 80, there is a great deal of private land in the vicinity. New gates, *No Trespassing* signs and *No mountain bikes* signs have begun to show up, closing off routes to the public. The Pacific Crest Trail also crosses through this area, and it is always closed to mountain bikes. All rides in this section go through private land, but they are open to the public and you will find plenty of challenging rides to keep you busy.

Trailhead Location: All of the rides in this chapter start and end at Donner Memorial State Park (T17N, R16E, Section 18), located just off Interstate 80 on the shore of Donner Lake.

Campgrounds: The most popular place to stay here is Donner Memorial State Park, which is open June through September. Make reservations by calling MISTIX at 1-800-444-7275 or the State Park at (916) 587-3841. Three U.S. Forest Service Campgrounds—Silver Creek, Goose Meadows and Granite Flat—are located nearby on Highway 89 between Truckee and Tahoe City. Silver Creek has a water system, but at Goose Meadows and Granite Flat treated water is not available.

Seasons: June through October or until the first major Sierra snow-fall. Autumn is a peaceful time to visit the State Park and Museum, and the riding is fantastic after the first fall rain!

Nearest Services: Truckee should have all that you will need: bike shops, grocery stores, restaurants and gas stations.

#1   Tinker Knob Loop

Level of Difficulty: For experienced riders in good physical condition. The road to the top gains over 2,000 feet, mostly over very rideable terrain with a couple of short rocky sections that some people may have to walk. The downhill stretch includes over 6 miles of singletrack with sections of technical 4-wheel drive roads. The downhill definitely makes the uphill worthwhile!

Mileage: 25 miles.

Elevation: 5,870 ft. to 8,200 ft.

Water: Water is available at several locations along the trail. Be sure to filter or treat all water from mountain streams. Treated water is available at Donner Memorial State Park and Silver Creek Campground.

Topo Maps: Unfortunately, this ride requires four maps! Norden, Truckee, Granite Chief and Tahoe City 7.5 min., or Tahoe, Truckee, Granite Chief and Donner Pass 15 min.

0.0 mile - From Donner State Park turn right on Donner Pass Road. Ride across Interstate 80 and through a couple of blocks of the town of Truckee. (Fill up your tires to maximum inflation for the first 8 miles of pavement!) 1.6 miles - Turn right on Highway 89, which takes you back under Interstate 80 and then along the Truckee River. 8.3 miles - Continue ahead and ride 1.6 miles past Goose Meadows Campground, then turn right on Forest Service Road 08. As you turn, you pass a sign that reads: *Begin 08.* 0.2 mile later, the road turns to dirt. 10.2 miles - Stay on the main road (Forest Service Road 08) that goes up and then down to a bridge. Cross the bridge and continue on the main road. 11.7 miles - Turn left at the intersection, following the sign to Upper Pole Creek. *Warning! The road straight ahead might seem like it heads in the right direction, but you will end up in Deep Creek Canyon instead of Pole Creek Canyon—and do a lot of climbing before the road ends!*

14 miles - Several roads will take off to the left to Upper Pole Creek. Stay on the main road. Soon you will arrive at a meadow, and the scenic part of the ride begins! All around you to the west are gigantic, rocky lava mountains. When you reach an intersection, stay to the right and continue uphill. 14.8 miles - As you go around the

Scenic riding in the Tahoe high country

ridge, the climbing is over for a short distance and the road drops quickly into Upper Deep Creek Canyon. Tinker Knob is to the west. Cross the creek and start the final climb to the top. There is one section near the top that most people have to walk. 17.2 miles - Turn right at the top of the ridge on an old jeep road, which is now just a trail. (Off to the left the road continues on as a trail to the top of Tinker Knob. You may want to ride or hike up it a bit to get a better look at the mountains around you.) Rest if you need to; it is all downhill from this point! When you are ready, start down the trail. It is very rocky and technical at first.

18.5 miles - The trail crosses the South Fork of Coldstream Creek, and the terrain gets easier as you enter the forest. Continue on. The trail becomes a road. 21 miles - When you reach the railroad tracks, look across and to the left for the main road. Listen for trains, then carefully cross over to the road and continue on through Coldstream Valley. Much of the valley is private land, so respect the *No Trespassing* signs and stay on the main road. When you reach the ponds, stay to the left on the main road. 24.4 miles - You ride through a gate. A short distance farther and to the left is a split rail fence that marks the boundary of Donner Memorial State Park. If you are staying in the

Park, take the trail just to the side of the fence near site 101 in Creek Campground. If you are not staying at the Park, continue straight ahead to Donner Pass Road.

#2   Coldstream Valley

Level of Difficulty: Good beginner ride. Most of the terrain is gradual uphill, with one or two short, steep climbs. The farther up Coldstream Canyon you ride, the tougher the riding gets. Most beginners will want to turn around a half-mile or so past the railroad crossing.
Mileage: 8 miles out and back to Horseshoe Bend.
Elevation: 5,900 ft. to 6,230 ft.
Topo Maps: Norden and Truckee 7.5 min., or Donner Pass and Truckee 15 min.

0.0 mile - If you are staying at Donner State Park, ride past site 101 in Creek Campground and look for a sign for an overflow parking area (on the other side of the wooden fence you can see the road heading to Coldstream Valley). Take the trail to the left that leads to the road going into Coldstream Valley. If you are not staying at the Park, turn south off Donner Pass Road just east of the State Park and follow the signs to Coldstream Valley. 0.2 mile - When you reach the park boundary, stay on the main road that bears left through the middle gate (there are three gates), and continue on. After one steep uphill it levels out. Continue on the main road that passes on the right side of two ponds, then gradually climbs up through the valley. The majority of the valley is private land, so stay on the main road.

3.6 miles - The road brings you to Horseshoe Bend, a spot where the Southern Pacific Railroad makes a sharp turn around the end of the valley. Beginners may want to quit here, but if you would like to ride farther, cross the tracks and continue on. The first mile past the tracks is not too difficult, but if you go much farther you will see why Ride #1 comes down this way instead of up! When you are done exploring, follow your tracks back to the park.

#3   Lakeview Canyon Loop

Level of Difficulty: Easy intermediate ride. There is a steady climb in the beginning, but nothing very technical. It's a fun, short ride with good scenery.
Mileage: 11 miles.
Elevation: 5,960 ft. to 6,840 ft.
Topo Maps: Norden and Truckee 7.5 min., or Donner Pass and Truckee 15 min.

Careful creek crossing

0.0 mile - From Donner State Park, ride west through the park along the shore. 1.4 miles - Go around the two gates that mark the western boundary of the Park, and continue riding west on South Shore Drive. 2.7 miles - Turn left on Lakeview Canyon Road. It is hard to find, but if you look carefully you will see a brown Forest Service sign, *Lakeview Canyon*. The road starts off steep, then eases up the rest of the way into the canyon. 3.4 miles - Stay right on the main road and continue climbing. 3.8 miles - Go left and finish the climb up to the railroad tracks. (The right turn also goes to the tracks, but the left is more direct.)

4.2 miles - When you reach the railroad tracks, turn right on the road that follows along the tracks. 4.8 miles - As the railroad tracks begin to curve into Lakeview Canyon, look across the tracks for the power lines. Ride a short distance past the lines and then carefully cross the tracks. Look for a trail that goes up the hill next to the remains of an old building. Follow this trail to the top of the saddle. (It becomes a road on the way up.) 5.0 miles - From the top you can see Squaw Peak and the mountains of Granite Chief Wilderness to the south. 5.4 miles - Turn left at the intersection. You are now riding on the Truckee River Route of Old Emigrant Trail.

6.3 miles - When the road forks, stay right and cross Emigrant Creek. (The creek may be dry by late August.) 6.8 miles - Turn left and ride over to the railroad tracks in Horseshoe Bend. Listen for trains and cross when it is safe. Continue on the main road that goes through Coldstream Valley. (For more details on the next stretch, see Ride #2.) 10.3 miles - After leaving Coldstream Valley, you arrive at a gate that may be open or closed. Go around the gate and continue on. If you are staying at the park, you can enter the campground on the trail next to the split rail fence ahead. If you parked at the entrance, continue riding out the paved road, turn left by the gas stations on Donner Pass Road, and ride back to your car.

#4   Old Emigrant Trail to Donner Peak

Level of Difficulty: Strong intermediate or better riding skills. Scenic high country ride with a fun downhill on singletrack trail and old jeep roads. Some people may have to walk a few short sections of the uphill, but never for very long. A good ride for enjoying fall colors, this route follows a section of the Old Emigrant Trail, which was first marked in 1924.
Mileage: 18.5 miles.

Singletrack through the forest

Elevation: 5,940 ft. to 7,840 ft.
Water: Water is available at Donner Memorial State Park. Late in the summer you may not reach water again for 12 miles (Cold Creek). Be sure to filter or treat all water you take from streams.
Topo Maps: Norden and Truckee 7.5 min., or Donner Pass and Truckee 15 min.

0.0 mile - From Donner Memorial State Park, follow Ride #3 for the first 5.4 miles. Turn right on Old Emigrant Trail. The road is very rocky at first but smooths out as you begin the climb up Emigrant Canyon. Old Emigrant Trail is very well marked with a variety of older and newer signs. 6.2 miles - When you reach a small round meadow on your right, the road forks in several directions. Take the road that goes straight ahead, just to the left of the meadow. It turns into a trail, and you should still be following the old trail signs. In the next section there may be short uphills that some people will walk, but if the traction is good the uphill is all rideable.

7.6 miles - As you reach a saddle at the base of Mount Judah, the trail again becomes a narrow road. The steep parts of the climb are over, and the road gradually climbs the rest of the way to Donner Peak. 8.9 miles - When Old Emigrant Trail reaches the saddle behind Donner Peak, look for the monument with a sign: *Emigrant Trail Truckee River Route - Highest Point on the Truckee Route - Elevation 7,850 ft.* From here there is a trail to the top of Donner Peak (elev. 8,019 ft.). Hike up to the top, enjoy the view, and prepare for the fun downhill ahead! When you are rested, follow your tracks back down to the intersection where you first got onto Old Emigrant Trail.

12.4 miles - When you reach the intersection, continue straight ahead on Old Emigrant Trail. 13.4 miles - Stay right and ride across Emigrant Creek. 13.9 miles - When the road ends, turn left and ride up to the railroad tracks. Cross when it is safe and continue on the main road through Coldstream Valley. Stay to the left when you reach the ponds. 17.4 miles - After you leave Coldstream Valley, you arrive at a gate that may be open or closed. Go around the gate and continue on. If you are staying in the park, you can enter the campground on the trail next to the split rail fence ahead. If you parked at the entrance, continue riding out the paved road, turn left by the gas stations on Donner Pass Road, and ride back to your car.

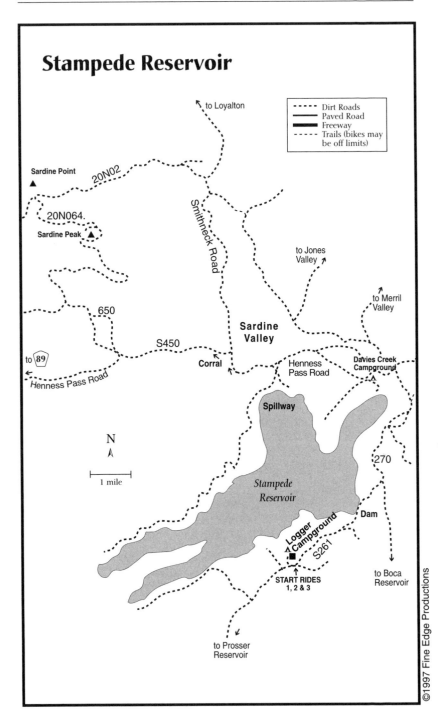

Stampede Reservoir

to Loyalton

Dirt Roads
Paved Road
Freeway
Trails (bikes may
be off limits)

Sardine Point

20N02

20N064.

Sardine Peak

Smithneck Road

to Jones
Valley

to Merril
Valley

650

S450

**Sardine
Valley**

to 89

Henness Pass Road

Corral

Henness
Pass Road

**Davies Creek
Campground**

Spillway

N

1 mile

*Stampede
Reservoir*

270

Dam

Logger
Campground

S261

**START RIDES
1, 2 & 3**

to Boca
Reservoir

to Prosser
Reservoir

©1997 Fine Edge Productions

CHAPTER 6

᚛🚲᚜

Stampede/Sardine Peak

The Stampede/Sardine Peak area, located to the north of Truckee and east of Highway 89 at the edge of the Tahoe and Toiyabe National Forests, features miles of dirt roads winding through large aspen groves, past giant juniper trees, and through meadows and small valleys following numerous creeks. This is a place for those who enjoy longer rides on good dirt roads with only a few rocky sections. The road system is well signed, which should give most mountain bikers the confidence to explore on their own beyond the rides mentioned here.

The best time to visit is in spring, when the meadows are bright green and full of wildflowers. Come in the fall to enjoy the colors of the aspen and cottonwood groves. It can get very warm here in the middle of the summer.

Seasons: May through October or until the first major snowstorm.

STAMPEDE RESERVOIR

Stampede is the largest of three reservoirs located within this area. All three reservoirs–Boca, Prosser and Stampede–have campgrounds along the shore and are good places for boating, fishing and mountain biking. This is a popular summer recreation area, and the campgrounds are usually full on weekends.

Stampede and Prosser Reservoirs were developed right over the Truckee River Route of the Old Emigrant Trail, a route used by pioneers including the Donner Party. If you enjoy history, be sure to visit the Donner Camp Picnic Area near Prosser Reservoir on Highway 89. There is a good historical interpretive trail, and you can easily ride there by mountain bike from any of the campgrounds.

Trailhead Location: All of the rides in this section start from Logger Campground at Stampede Reservoir (24 miles east of Truckee), T19N, R17E Section 30. Take I-80 east for 6.5 miles, then get off at the Hirshdale exit and follow the signs to Stampede Reservoir. The rides can also be done from any of the campgrounds within the area by riding to the end of the pavement on County Road 270.

Topo Maps: Boca, Sardine Peak, Dog Valley and Hobart Mills 7.5 min., or Truckee and Loyalton 15 min. All rides use the same maps.

Campgrounds: There are USFS campgrounds at all three reservoirs. A small undeveloped campground, Davis Creek, is located at the east end of Stampede Reservoir. Davis Creek does not have a water system, and the creek can be dry by late summer. Camping is allowed only within designated areas.

Nearest Services: The town of Truckee, at the intersection of Highway 89 and Interstate 80, should have everything you need: grocery stores, restaurants and bike shops.

#1 North Shore

Level of Difficulty: Intermediate ride with very little elevation change. Great for a picnic ride to the far side of the reservoir. Beginners may choose to turn around before reaching the Little Truckee River, 11 miles out.
Mileage: 24 miles out and back.

0.0 mile - From Logger Campground, turn left on S261. Ride across the dam and continue to County Road 270. 2.0 miles -Turn left on County Road 270. Ride through Hoke Valley to the far end of Stampede Reservoir. 4.0 miles - When the pavement ends at a "T," turn left on Henness Pass Road (County Road S860). A right on Henness Pass Road leads to Dog Valley, another area with many dirt roads to explore by mountain bike. 4.6 miles - Stay right on the main road, following the signs to Sardine Valley.

5.6 miles - When you reach Sardine Valley, turn left and stay on the main road (County Road 2860). 6.3 miles - Turn left at a triangular intersection. Ride up a small hill and look for the Forest Service sign that reads: *Day use only beyond this point.* Continue on this road, which takes you back along the north shore of Stampede Reservoir to several nice picnic spots. The upper end of the reservoir, where the Little Truckee River enters, is 5.5 miles farther out (11.8 miles total). Enjoy your picnic by the reservoir, and then follow your tracks back to the campground. (If you are looking for a longer ride, the road continues on from here to Kyburz Flat and loops back into Henness Pass Road.)

#2   Sardine Peak Lookout Loop

Level of Difficulty: All day distance ride for strong intermediate riders or better. The roads are all good surface dirt, with only a few rocky sections. The uphill climb of over 2,000 feet is done over several miles and is all rideable.
Mileage: 31 miles.
Elevation: 6,000 ft. to 8,135 ft.
Water: Water is available at Logger Campground and at several creeks along the way. Be sure to filter or treat all water you take from mountain streams.

0.0 mile - Follow Ride #1 for the first 6.3 miles. At that point, continue straight ahead on the main road which heads west and then turns north along the edge of Sardine Valley. 7.3 miles - Turn left on County Road S450 which begins to climb as you enter Davis Canyon. 9.1 miles - Turn right on Lemon Canyon Road (County Road 650). (The road to the left goes to Highway 89, 8 miles away.) 10.5 miles - Turn right at the sign: *Sardine Lookout 4 miles.* The next 4 miles are a steady climb, and you gain 1,500 feet up to the top of the ridge. 14.2 miles - Turn left and continue the last short climb to the lookout tower.

Road into Sardine Valley

14.5 miles - From the top you can see your starting point, Stampede Reservoir, with Boca Reservoir in the distance and Sardine Valley below. To the southwest are the higher peaks of the Sierra Nevada and Donner Lake. The jagged peaks to the northwest are the Sierra Buttes. When you are through enjoying the view, ride back down to the last intersection. 14.8 miles - Turn left on 20N64.1. (You came up the road that is to your right.) 16.4 miles - Turn right on 20N02 and get ready for some downhill fun. 16.9 miles - As you descend, be on the lookout for two huge western juniper trees. The one on the right has a sign stating that it is one of the largest specimens living today. Continue downhill into Trosi Canyon, which is full of aspen and cottonwood trees. This section is spectacular in the fall when all the leaves are yellow, orange and gold! 18.8 miles - Continue past the gate. Be sure to leave it how you found it (open if it was open and closed if it was closed).

18.9 miles - Stay to the right on the main road. 19.7 miles - When you reach Sardine Valley, turn right on Smithneck Road, following the signs to Stampede Reservoir. 19.9 miles - The road forks as you reach the north end of Sardine Valley. Either fork will take you back to Stampede Reservoir. (These directions continue to the right on Smithneck Road.) 23 miles - County Road S450 takes off to your right, and you are back at the 7.3 mile point. From here, follow your tracks back to the campground.

#3 Sardine Valley Loop

Level of Difficulty: A long, scenic ride for strong beginners—a loop around Sardine Valley.
Mileage: 19 miles.
Elevation: 6,000 ft. to 6,360 ft.
Water: Water is available at Logger Campground and at several creeks along the way. (Be sure to filter or treat the water.) Many of the creeks may be dry late in the summer or fall.

0.0 mile - Follow Ride #2 for the first 7.3 miles. From here Ride #2 turns left, but this ride continues straight ahead to complete the loop around Sardine Valley.

10.4 miles - Turn right at the north end of Sardine Valley. The road goes along the east side of the valley following the power lines. You ride past two roads on the left that go up over the ridge to Jones Valley and Merril Valley. 14.6 miles - Continue on the main road which leaves Sardine Valley and Davis Creek before turning south. When the road ends, turn left on Henness Pass Road. 14.9 miles - Turn right on the paved road and continue back to the campground.

BEAR VALLEY CAMPGROUND

Trailhead Location: All rides in this section begin at Bear Valley Campground, T20N, R16E, Section 30. To get to Bear Valley Campground from Truckee, drive 14 miles north on Highway 89 to the intersection of County Road 451 and Forest Road 07. (Forest Road 07 goes to Jackson Meadows Reservoir, which is covered in Chapter 3.) Turn right on County Road 451, Lemon Canyon Road (partially paved), and drive 5.4 miles farther to Bear Valley Campground. Much of the forest in this vicinity was destroyed by fire in the mid-1990s, including most of the trees around, but not in, the campground.

Campgrounds: The smaller Bear Valley Campground is a good place to camp except during the hottest part of summer. (There are no streams or lakes for swimming.) Drinking water is available at the campground, but in late fall it may be turned off for the winter. Two campgrounds—Lower Little Truckee and Upper Little Truckee—are located 11 miles north of Truckee on Highway 89. Both are on the Little Truckee River and both have water systems. The rides in this section can also be done from these two campgrounds. Just follow the directions given for driving to Bear Valley Campground. This will add 14 miles—7 miles each way—to your trips.

Nearest Services: There are small stores and gas stations in Sierraville, north on Highway 89. Larger stores, restaurants and bike shops can be found in Truckee.

#4   Sardine Peak Lookout from Bear Valley

Level of Difficulty: Intermediate level hill climb. The road surfaces are all good dirt with only a few short, rocky sections. Beginners in good physical condition should enjoy this ride.

Mileage: 13 miles for the loop; 10 miles to Sardine Lookout out and back.

Elevation: 6,594 ft. to 8,135 ft.

Topo Maps: Sardine Peak 7.5 min., or Loyalton 15 min.

0.0 mile - From Bear Valley Campground, ride southeast out Lemon Canyon Road (County Road 650). It is signed *Sardine Lookout 5 miles*—

Sardine Valley 7 miles. For a mile or so, you ride through a heavily burned area. 1.6 miles - Turn left and follow the signs to Sardine Lookout. If you ride the loop, you will return to this intersection. From here the road gets steeper as you climb up to Sardine Point. 2.9 mile - When you reach the top of the ridge, turn right on Road 20N64.1 and keep following the signs to Sardine Lookout. After a flat section the road goes up again with one rocky area. Several roads take off from the main road and most of them are clearly marked *Dead End Road.* Just remember to stay on the main road that continues climbing to the Lookout.

4.4 miles - The road straight ahead—County Road 650—goes to Davis Canyon, and when you complete the loop you will return to this point. Turn right, following the sign to the Lookout. 4.7 miles - From the top of Sardine Peak (elev. 8,135 ft.), you

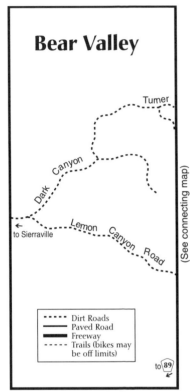

Bear Valley

Tumer

Canyon

Dark

Lemon Canyon Road

← to Sierraville

(See connecting map)

- - - - Dirt Roads
——— Paved Road
▬▬▬ Freeway
- - - - Trails (bikes may be off limits)

to 89

©1997 Fine Edge Productions

can enjoy a 360° view. Unfortunately the bottom stairs are missing from the lookout tower, but the view is good from the ground, too. To the southeast you can see Sardine Valley, Stampede Reservoir and Boca Reservoir; to the southwest is Donner Lake surrounded by mountains. To the northwest, the jagged peaks you see sticking up from the forest are Sierra Buttes. After you enjoy the view, your choices are to ride back the way you came or follow the directions for the loop.

5.0 miles - To finish the loop ride, turn right and follow the sign that reads: *Davis Canyon 6 miles.* Follow the main road that goes out on the ridge, makes a big switchback, and heads downhill into a small valley. 8.7 miles - When you reach the valley, turn right on County Road 650, Lemon Canyon Road, which winds its way along a creek and takes you through a large meadow. 11.1 miles - You are back at the intersection where the road on the right heads to Sardine Lookout. Continue straight ahead and follow your tracks back to the campground.

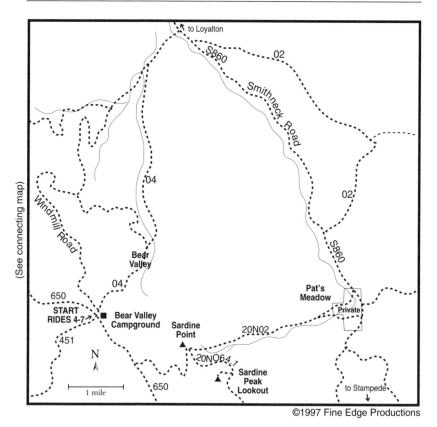

©1997 Fine Edge Productions

#5   Western Juniper Loop

On the Juniper Loop you will ride past a very large western juniper tree that is signed: *Western Juniper · Juniperus occidentalis.* With a circumference of 30 feet, this specimen represents one of the largest known trees of its species. You will be rapidly descending when you pass the juniper, so be sure to pay attention and look to your right when you get to the downhill on the northeast side of Sardine Peak.

Level of Difficulty: Intermediate all-day ride. The entire ride is on good surface dirt roads with two miles of pavement.
Mileage: 20.5 miles (24.5 miles if you ride to the top of Sardine Lookout).
Elevation: 6,594 ft. to 8,135 ft.
Water: Water is available at Bear Valley Campground and at several creeks along the way. (Be sure to filter or treat all water from streams.) There is also water at Loyalton, 17 miles into the ride.
Topo Maps: Sardine Peak and Loyalton 7.5 min., or Loyalton 15 min.

0.0 mile - Follow Ride #4 for the first 2.9 miles to the top of the ridge by Sardine Point. At that point, continue straight ahead on 20N02 instead of turning right and riding to the Lookout. (For a longer ride, detour out to the Lookout for the view and return to this intersection to continue. This adds 4 miles to the loop.) 3.4 miles - As you descend, be sure to look for two large western juniper trees, one on each side of the road. The one on the right has the sign on it. Continue on down into Trosi Canyon, which is full of aspens and cottonwoods. (This is a spectacular ride for seeing fall color!)

5.3 miles - There is a gate across the road. Continue on, making sure to leave the gate how you found it (closed if closed, open if open). 5.4 miles - Stay to the right on the main road. (The road to the left goes to the same place, but since it crosses private land, it is best to stay to the right here.) 6.2 miles - When you reach Sardine Valley, turn left on Smithneck Road. (The road to the right goes to Stampede Reservoir.) Continue on past Pat's Meadow. 6.9 miles - The road to Babbitt Lookout (6 miles) takes off to your right, in case you are looking for another ride to try! Continue on the main road that follows Smithneck Creek through more aspen groves and past several good picnic and rest spots. If you look closely, you should see beaver dams all along the creek.

This burn at Bear Valley Campground occurred in the mid-1990s

12 miles - The road, now marked County Road S860, turns to pavement. Continue on. Soon you pass a small memorial picnic spot. This is a nice shady area if you need a break. 13.5 miles - At the edge of the town of Loyalton, turn left on Bear Valley Road. 13.9 miles - The pavement ends and the road gets rough for a short distance. Continue following the signs to Bear Valley Campground. You pass several roads that head west (right), some of which are included in other rides in this chapter. There are several other options for loop rides in this area, and all you need to do is pay attention to the road signs and carry a good map.

15.1 miles - Stay to the left as the road begins to climb along Bear Valley Creek. 18.1 miles - The road enters Bear Valley, another large meadow. Continue through the valley and follow the signs back to Bear Valley Campground, another 2.4 miles.

#6   Bear Valley

Level of Difficulty: Easy, short beginner ride on narrow, well-groomed dirt road.
Mileage: 5 miles out and back.
Elevation: 6,280 ft. to 6,394 ft.

Most of this ride is through a forested area that was blackened by fire. 0.0 mile - From Bear Valley Campground, ride north on Forest Road 04, which rolls along gently climbing and descending small hills to Bear Valley. Ride out to the far end of the valley (2 miles). When you are done exploring, follow your tracks back to the campground.

#7   Turner Canyon Loop

Level of Difficulty: Intermediate level ride for people in good physical condition. The road gains and loses elevation over and over, but none of the climbs require walking. Good spring and fall ride.
Mileage: Turner Canyon Loop is 18 miles; Windmill Road Loop is 13.2 miles.
Elevation: 6,594 ft. to 5,440 ft. to 6,570 ft. to 5,400 ft. to 6,594 ft. Total elevation gain: 2,324 ft.
Water: Water is available at Bear Valley Campground and at several creeks along the ride. Be sure to filter or treat all water taken from mountain streams.
Topo Maps: Sardine Peak and Sierraville 7.5 min., or Loyalton 15 min.

0.0 mile - From Bear Valley Campground, ride north on Forest Road 04. Stay on the main road that goes through Bear Valley and continues into a small canyon following Bear Valley Creek. 5.2 miles - Turn left on the Turner Canyon Road at the sign reading: *Turner Canyon 1 mile - Lemon Canyon 8 miles.* 5.8 miles - Windmill Road takes off to the left. This is an option for a shorter loop back to Bear Valley. (Just stay on Windmill Road and follow the signs 6 miles back to Bear Valley or 8 miles back to the campground.) To finish the Turner Canyon Loop, continue on the main road that begins to climb as it enters Turner Canyon.

8.8 miles - The road levels out on top of Bear Flat, then starts back down the west side into Dark Canyon. 13.2 miles - Turner Canyon ends at Lemon Canyon Road (County Road 650). Turn left. The road begins to climb again as you ride through Lemon Canyon, which is filled with aspens. Stay on the main road that takes you back to Bear Valley Campground (4.5 miles).

Pavement ride through the forest

CHAPTER 7

🚲

Foresthill/French Meadows

The Foresthill area, located 18 miles east of Auburn, covers a wide variety of terrain from steep, rocky, river canyons lined with oak trees to the high country of Granite Chief Wilderness Area. The Foresthill area, now sparsely populated, was once full of booming gold mining towns. You will be riding on old trails with historical names like "Last Chance," trails that were at one time toll routes. Everywhere you look there are signs of mining that took place here in the 1850s.

These rides all start from different locations along the Forest Hill Road, which follows Forest Hill Divide. From Sacramento, drive east on Interstate 80 to Auburn. Take the Foresthill exit and continue to Foresthill. At the eastern edge of town where the road forks, stay left on Forest Hill Road.

Campgrounds: Several U.S. Forest Service Campgrounds are located along, or a short distance from, the Forest Hill Road. Secret House and Robinsons Flats are "undeveloped" campgrounds (no piped in water). Nicer campgrounds can be found at Sugar Pine Reservoir and at French Meadows Reservoir.

Seasons: Mid-May through October. See the individual rides for more details.

Nearest Services: The town of Foresthill should have all that you need in the way of grocery stores, gas stations and a few restaurants. The closest bike shops are back in Auburn.

WESTERN STATES 100

The Western States 100 is an annual ultra-marathon running event which has become one of the best known in the country. To qualify as a finisher you must run the entire 100 miles in under 30 hours.

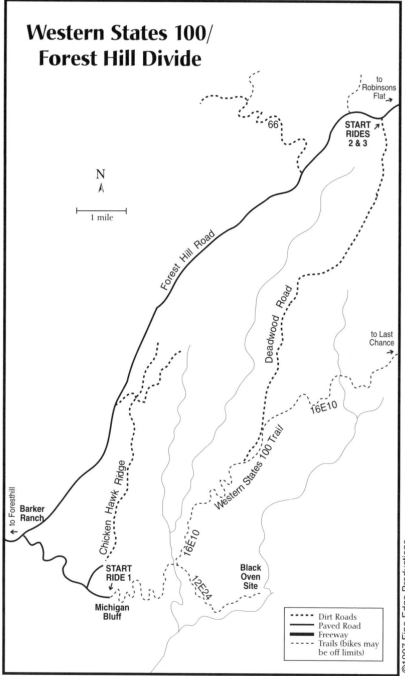

Western States 100/
Forest Hill Divide

to Robinsons Flat

66

START RIDES 2 & 3

N

1 mile

Forest Hill Road

Deadwood Road

to Last Chance

16E10

Western States 100 Trail

Chicken Hawk Ridge

to Foresthill

Barker Ranch

16E10

START RIDE 1

12E24

Black Oven Site

Michigan Bluff

Dirt Roads
Paved Road
Freeway
Trails (bikes may be off limits)

©1997 Fine Edge Productions

Runners start in Squaw Valley, climb up and over Emigrant Pass (elev. 8,760 ft.), and finish in Auburn (1,300 ft.). This doesn't sound too bad until you look at the specifics of the race where the actual elevation gain is over 17,000 feet, elevation loss over 21,000 feet. This is an extremely tough, challenging course. Much of the Western States 100 Trail lies within Tahoe National Forest, and a large portion is open to mountain bikes. The only part of the trail on National Forest land closed to moun-

Last Chance Trail Marker

tain bikes is that which goes through Granite Chief Wilderness Area.

Many of the rides included in this section will take you on the Western States 100 and follow the route for a few miles. Be sure to read the ride descriptions. This is tough, rugged, isolated country and very challenging mountain bike riding. The rest of the trail is marked on the Tahoe National Forest Map, and if you enjoyed these shorter sections you may want to try some others.

#1   El Dorado Canyon Loop

The El Dorado Canyon Loop follows along the route of the Western States 100 Endurance Race. This is one of the most challenging rides in this guidebook.

To get to the start from Foresthill, drive out Forest Hill Road 4.5 miles to Baker Ranch. Turn right on the Michigan Bluff road. 2.9 miles farther you will reach the gold rush town of Michigan Bluff. Limited parking is available in front of the homes here. To conserve parking space, the locals like you to park straight in rather than parallel.

Level of Difficulty: Advanced riders only! *Do not try this ride alone.* Depending on the time of year, it could be days before anyone else ventures down the trail. Be sure you feel comfortable with the ability of all riders that go with you. If someone gets hurt it will be up to your group to evacuate them or ride out for help. All rescues must be done on foot. Have fun, enjoy the downhill, but ride carefully! Watch out for rattlesnakes in the canyon and poison oak all along the trail section.

Mileage: 31 miles.

Elevation: 1,800 ft. to 5,400 ft. The ride starts at 3,500 feet, climbs to 5,400 feet, descends to 1,800 feet, and climbs back to 3,500 feet.

Water: No water is available at the start of the ride, so be sure your bottles are full when you leave Foresthill. The only water on the ride is at the 27-mile point in El Dorado Canyon. Be sure to filter or treat all water taken from mountain streams.

The view from Forest Hill Road

Seasons: Mid-May through October. Spring and fall (after the first rains) are the best times to do this ride. Avoid the middle of the summer when the canyon is very hot and dry.
Topo Maps: Michigan Bluff and Westville 7.5 min., or Duncan Peak 15 min.
Trailhead Location: Michigan Bluff, T14N, R11E, Section 22.

0.0 mile - From Michigan Bluff ride back up the paved road you drove in on. 0.6 mile - When you come to a sign that reads *Community of the Great Commission 1/2,* turn right on Chicken Hawk Road, which starts off paved. Several roads will go left and right; just stay on the main road that goes northeast out the ridge. 1.2 miles - Stay right on Chicken Hawk Road, which becomes a dirt road. The road continues to climb back up on the ridge. If you look off in the distance to the right, you will see the Crystal Range of the Sierra Nevada. 5.5 miles - Chicken Hawk Road ends at wide, paved Forest Hill Road. Turn right. For the next 10 miles you ride along the paved road. It is steady, but never steep, as you gain 1,200 feet before going slightly downhill to Deadwood Ridge. This part of the ride is scenic and not difficult, but many may prefer to do the shuttle option described in Ride #2 to avoid riding 10 miles of pavement.

15.3 miles - Turn right on Deadwood Road. Take a break in the shade and prepare for the downhill! First the road takes you gradually down Deadwood Ridge, but it gets steeper and your speed increases. 21.6 miles - Continue on Deadwood Road, passing the Western States 100 Trail that goes east to Devils Thumb. 23.3 miles - Go left on the Western States 100 Trail. Deadwood Road heads to the right and ends up at the same place, but the trail is more fun to ride. 24.2 miles - The Western States 100 Trail and Deadwood Road meet again at the Deadwood Cemetery. This old cemetery from the Gold Rush days is all that is left of a town. From here the loop continues down the trail to the left. Please read the warning posted on the trail sign! The trail is not well maintained from this point on; it is very steep and narrow, and it is also open to motorcycles, hikers and horseback riders. *Caution: If you are tired do not proceed! Once you ride down into the canyon the only way out is by bicycle or by foot. If someone is injured it will be up to your group to get help or manage the rescue alone.*

The trail–historically known as the "Last Chance Trail"–quickly begins to drop off into El Dorado Canyon. If you try this ride in the fall after the first rain the big leaf maple trees will be yellow and the air will be filled with the strong scent of bay trees that line the trail.

This is a fun, technical section, and all your efforts will be concentrated on negotiating the route. Plan to stop occasionally to shake out your hands and enjoy the view! *Watch out for poison oak the entire way down, and rattlesnakes the closer you get to the river!*

27.7 miles - Cross the bridge over El Dorado Canyon. Below the bridge there is a good swimming hole and a nice place to take a break in the shade. If you are out of water be sure to resupply here. *(Filter or treat all water taken from the river.)* Don't be fooled by the map and assume you are almost back to the car—it's a 3,500-foot climb and a thirsty 3.5 miles away. For many this still won't sound too tough, but the trail winds its way out onto south-facing slopes with very little shade.

When you are rested, start up the trail. There is an old jeep road here too, but it is steeper than the trail, so most people prefer to follow the Western States 100 Trail. If you haven't yet gained a new respect for long distance runners, this next section of trail may convince you! The first part of the climb is the steepest, but the worst part is when the trail heads out into the sunny spots on the south-facing slopes. If you start to feel tired, just think a moment about the runners making their way up out of the canyon. This is the 60 mile point in the race and the lead runners get here after running 10 to 11 hours!

Everyone will push in spots on this climb. Just remember it is only 3.5 miles to your car. Once the trail crosses the creek in Poor Mans Canyon, it becomes more rideable. When it merges with the road it's an easy ride the rest of the way back to your car.

#2   Deadwood to Michigan Bluff

Level of Difficulty: Strong intermediate to advanced riders. Be sure to read all the warnings mentioned in Ride #1. You will eliminate 15 miles of gradual climbing by doing this ride as a shuttle, but this does not reduce the degree of difficulty. You will only be less tired when you reach the tough sections.
Mileage: 16 miles.
Elevation: 5,400 ft. to 1,800 ft. to 3,500 ft.
Trailhead and Shuttle Locations: This is a shuttle ride requiring you to leave one car at Michigan Bluff and one at Deadwood Road. Follow the directions to Michigan Bluff in Ride #1. To get to the beginning of the ride from Foresthill, drive out Forest Hill Road 17 miles to Deadwood Road.

0.0 mile - Start riding at the beginning of Deadwood Road. Refer to Ride #1 for directions, starting at the 15.3 mile point. The total mileage one way will be 16 miles—12.5 miles of downhill with 3.5 miles of uphill at the end.

#3   Deadwood Cemetery

This is a good ride for less experienced mountain bikers who got talked into being the shuttle drivers for Ride #1, or for those who are curious about this ride and would like to see what the Western States 100 trail looks like.

Level of Difficulty: For intermediate or better riders. The ride follows a good dirt road all the way, with the option of trying a 1-mile section of the trail. Just remember, the first half of this ride is all downhill, so on the way back you do a lot of climbing.
Mileage: 17.8 miles out and back.
Elevation: 5,350 ft. to 3,900 ft.
Water: No water is available on this ride.
Trailhead Location: Intersection of Deadwood Road and Forest Hill Road (see directions in Ride #2).

0.0 mile - Ride out Deadwood Road from where it intersects Forest Hill Road. 6.3 miles - Continue straight ahead. (A road takes off to the left and goes to the Devil Thumb Check Point of the Western States Trail.) 8.0 miles - Here you can either stay right on Deadwood Road or go left and try a section of the Western States 100 Trail. 9.0 miles - The trail and the road meet at the Deadwood Cemetery. Rides #1 and #2 continue on the trail to the left. This ride ends here, and you might want to explore the old cemetery before heading back to your car.

#4   Robinsons Flat/Red Star Ridge Loop

Level of Difficulty: Advanced. This is an all-day adventure for experienced riders only. It's challenging, with lots of singletrack riding. The elevation profile only shows a total gain of about 1,800 feet, but in reality you will be gaining and losing elevation throughout the ride. Take along your topo maps for this ride.
Mileage: 22 miles.
Elevation: 6,700 ft. to 7,200 ft. to 5,400 ft. to 6,700 ft.
Water: Robinsons Flat Campground does not have a water system, but spring water is available. It is best to bring water with you from home. Out on the ride there is no water until you drop into Duncan Canyon 18 miles into the ride.
Seasons: June through October. We attempted to do this ride May 18th after a mild winter, and we were stopped by snow drifts before we even reached Robinsons Flat.
Topo Maps: Duncan Peak and Royal Gorge 7.5 min. or Duncan Peak and Granite Chief 15 min.
Trailhead Location: Robinson Flat Campground, T15N, R13E, Section 11. (See French Meadows map, p. 94.)

0.0 mile - From the Robinsons Flat Campground, continue out the county road (Foresthill/Soda Springs Road). It rolls along, gaining and losing elevation for a few miles, and then begins to climb back up as you ride around Sunflower Hill. After this it continues to gain and lose elevation once again. 6.5 miles - Turn right on Forest Road 96 at the intersection, following signs to French Meadows. (The main county road you have been riding continues all the way to Soda Springs on Interstate 80.) 7.9 miles - The road climbs to the top of the ridge at 7,213 feet. Continue to where a trail crosses the road and you see a sign: *13 miles Robinsons Flat - Tevis Cup Trail - PCT 11 miles*. Go right on Tevis Cup Trail, following the route of the Western States 100. The next 8 miles are all on challenging singletrack along Red Star Ridge. Don't think that it will be all downhill! Just like any ridge ride there are many great descents followed by some awesome climbs! You will gain a great respect for the runners who take part in the Western States Run! Most of this section of trail is rideable, but there are a couple of spots that almost everyone will have to push.

15.9 miles - At what appears to be the end of the ridge, turn right on the trail. (Going straight you would encounter a jeep road.) Ride the short, steep downhill and look straight ahead for the wooden signs on a tree: *Western States Trail - Robinsons Flat 6 miles*. Go right here toward Robinsons Flat. The trail gets tougher as it descends into Duncan Canyon. Then it climbs up out of one small canyon and drops down the other side before the final climb begins back up to Robinsons Flat. A series of switchbacks will help you gain the 1,300 feet to get out of Duncan Canyon. 22 miles - The trail ties into Foresthill/Soda Springs Road, which leads back to the campground.

SUGAR PINE RESERVOIR

Sugar Pine Reservoir Recreation Area is located north of Foresthill on the edge of the Tahoe National Forest. To get to the reservoir, drive northeast 9 miles on the Forest Hill Road and turn left (north) on Sugar Pine Road (Forest Road 10). Continue 6 miles on the paved road to the reservoir. Off to the right, just before you reach the reservoir, you will see the sign for the Parker Flat OHV Area. There is a small campground here, but the nicer one is located on the northwest shore of the reservoir. Other recreation here includes swimming, fishing and boating.

The following are just two examples of areas to ride in Sugar

Pine Recreation Area. This is one of those spots with an endless supply of dirt roads to explore.

Topo Maps: Dutch Flat 7.5 min., or Colfax 15 min. The area is in T15N, R10E, Section 24.

Campgrounds: There is a small "undeveloped" campground at the Parker Flat OHV Area. The better camping is on the north shore of Sugar Pine Reservoir. A group area camp is located on the southeast side of the reservoir and can be reserved by calling the Foresthill Ranger Station, (916) 367-2224.

Water: Water is available at the campgrounds, the picnic area, and at the boat launching area.

Seasons: The majority of the riding in this area is below 4,000 feet and can be ridden almost all year. The roads can sometimes be closed due to low elevation snow. If in doubt, call the Foresthill Ranger Station. The nicest times to visit are in spring and in fall after the first good rain. This area can be hot and dusty in the middle of the summer.

Nearest Services: Foresthill has grocery stores, gas stations and a few restaurants. The nearest bike shops are in Auburn.

#5   Sugar Pine Reservoir Loop

The path around Sugar Pine Reservoir is one of the first places that I have encountered a sign showing that the trail is designated for bicycle use. It was a pleasant surprise after a day's drive to find the trail and not have to worry if it was OK to ride it!

Please ride conservatively, especially on the paved sections near the campgrounds, since this area is also designated for wheelchair use. If you have any friends confined to a wheelchair, this is a nice spot to take them to enjoy the National Forest.

Level of Difficulty: Beginner. An easy, fun, well-maintained trail suitable for riders of all abilities, including children. It's very short, with only one set of switchbacks.
Mileage: 5 miles.
Trailhead Location: When you reach the reservoir, continue west, then north, to the largest campground (on the northwest shore of Sugar Reservoir).

0.0 mile - From the campground, ride toward the lake and find the paved trail. Ride southwest toward the dam, and soon the trail will turn to dirt. 0.8 mile - The trail has washed out and you will have to

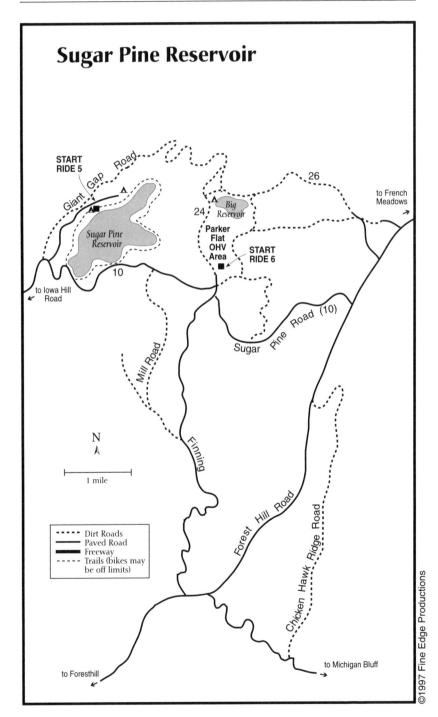

Sugar Pine Reservoir

START RIDE 5

Giant Gap Road

26

to French Meadows

24

Big Reservoir

Sugar Pine Reservoir

Parker Flat OHV Area

START RIDE 6

to Iowa Hill Road

10

Sugar Pine Road (10)

Mill Road

N

1 mile

Finning

Forest Hill Road

Chicken Hawk Ridge Road

- - - - - Dirt Roads
───── Paved Road
▬▬▬▬ Freeway
- - - - - Trails (bikes may be off limits)

to Foresthill

to Michigan Bluff

©1997 Fine Edge Productions

dismount and push your bike back up to the trail. 1.0 mile - You arrive at the dam and a small gate across the trail. It may not look like it at first, but the gate will swing open if you push on it. Ride across the dam and back out to the trail. Continuing around the lake shore, you pass the boat ramp and cross a bridge over Forbes Creek. Then you reach a small log bridge crossing Shirttail Creek that you may have to walk across. 4.2 mile - After crossing the bridge, continue the loop back to the campground.

#6   Parker Flats OHV Area

Parker Flats OHV Area is located just a half mile east of Sugar Pine Reservoir. There are over 30 miles of signed motorcycle and ATV trails to ride. All the trails are well marked and signed according to degree of difficulty. The easier trails are all rideable by mountain bike; the more difficult ones are fun, but you have to walk some of the steeper sections. You can ride your bike from the campgrounds at Sugar Pine Reservoir to this area and spend the day exploring the trails.

Warning: We visited in the fall on a week day after the first big rain, and no one was there at all. But we have been told that this OHV Area is heavily used on weekends. The Sugar Pine Area is great for riding in spring and fall, but not on a summer weekend!

FRENCH MEADOWS

French Meadows Recreation Area is located 40 miles east of Foresthill. This is a long way from anywhere, but once you arrive the riding is endless. It's a good place for a mountain bike retreat with a group. Other recreation includes boating, swimming and fishing. We saw one fisherman catch a 16" German Brown trout from the Middle Fork of the American River, which flows into French Meadows Reservoir. This area is on the western side of Granite Chief Wilderness Area, and it gets very little use. You can ride to the Wilderness boundary, park your bike, and then enjoy an easy hike into Picayune Valley, which has rocks with Indian petroglyphs. Much of the land lies within a State Game Refuge, so firearms are not allowed. This makes it a great place to try if you are worried about riding during hunting season.

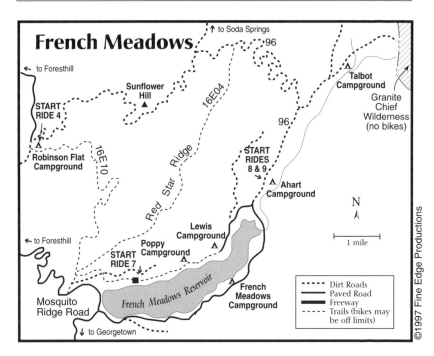

Topo Maps: Bunker Hill, Royal Gorge and Granite Chief 7.5 min., or Granite Chief 15 min.

Campgrounds: Camping is allowed only within designated campgrounds. French Meadows Campground and Lewis Campground—both on the shores of French Meadows Reservoir—are "full service" facilities with tables, toilets and piped water. Usually these campgrounds are full only on the three big summer weekends: Memorial Day, Fourth of July and Labor Day. Another nice campground is Ahart, located one mile upstream from the reservoir on the Middle Fork of the American River. Ahart has only 12 sites, and during the week we were the only people staying there. Water must be filtered from the stream. Several group camps are available by reservation only; call the Foresthill Ranger Station at (619) 367-2224.

Nearest Services: Fill your gas tank when you leave Georgetown or Foresthill. It is better to drive a truck than a car in this area. There are no services available, so take all the food, beverages and ice you think you will need. Prepare to be completely self-sufficient, since the nearest bike shops are in Placerville or Auburn.

#7   Poppy Trail

Level of Difficulty: Intermediate skill level. You should know how to move your
bike around rocks, or you will have to walk through the creek drainages.
Mileage: 6 miles out and back.
Elevation: 5,200 to 5,400 ft.
Trailhead Location: The Poppy Trail—otherwise known as the McGuire Trail—is
located on the north shore of French Meadows Reservoir. Either drive or ride your
bike along the north shore, following signs to McGuire Picnic Area.

0.0 mile - From the McGuire Picnic Area Entrance, turn right into the
picnic area and continue toward the restroom. 0.2 mile - Turn right at
the sign which reads: *Trail to Western States Trail - 3 miles to dam - 1 mile to
Poppy Campground.* Follow the road to the trailhead. The McGuire Trail
is a 3-mile route that leads along the shore to the spillway. 1.2 miles -
You reach Poppy Campground, a small area for boaters, bikers and
hikers. This is a fun stretch of singletrack that doesn't seem to get
much use, especially past Poppy Campground. Watch out for hikers
and be careful crossing the creek drainages. 2.9 miles - When you
reach the spillway, turn around and ride the same trail back.

Ride #8   Granite Chief Bike and Hike

Level of Difficulty: Easy. Riding out and back to the Wilderness Boundary is
suitable for beginners, including older children. The addition of the hike to
Picayune Valley would be too much for small children, but for others it makes a
fun, all-day adventure. Pack a lunch if you decide to add the hike to your bike trip!
Mileage: 10 miles out and back from Talbot Campground. Bike and hike to
Picayune Valley for 19 miles total.
Elevation: 5,300 ft. to 5,800 ft.
Trailhead Location: Ahart Campground.

0.0 mile - Starting from Ahart Campground, go east on Forest Road 96
and follow the Middle Fork of the American River. 2.0 miles - Continue
straight on 16E10. (Road 96 goes uphill and to the left.) There is a sign
for Forest Hill Divide, Soda Springs, and Foresthill. 3.0 miles - Continue straight ahead. The road to the right goes to Dobbas Cow Camp
(private land). 3.5 miles - Go right, following the sign for Talbot Campground and Granite Chief Wilderness. 4.0 miles - You arrive at Talbot
Campground and are faced with a Vehicle Control Gate at the creek.
No motor vehicles are allowed beyond this point. Go around the gate

and across the stream; then continue on the main road.

5.0 miles - You arrive at the Granite Chief Wilderness boundary (*No Bikes Allowed!*). Here you can leave your bikes and hike into the Wilderness Area. An easy day hike of 4.5 miles will bring you to Picayune Valley, a narrow valley surrounded by rock cliffs. Look closely and you may find petroglyphs on the rock walls. This is also supposed to be a great area for fishing. When you are through exploring, hike back to your bikes and ride back to the campground.

Ride #9   Red Star Ridge Loop

Level of Difficulty: Advanced riders will enjoy the challenge of this ride. With nearly 2,000 feet of climbing, it is not a ride for beginners! The trail section follows the route of the Western States 100 Race and is very technical.
Mileage: 22 miles.
Elevation: 5,330 ft. to 7,180 ft.
Water: Carry all that you think you will need. Red Star Ridge can be hot and dry. There is no water until you return to French Meadows Reservoir, 18 miles into the ride. Be sure to filter or treat all the water you take from lakes or streams.
Trailhead Location: Ahart Campground.

0.0 mile - Starting from Ahart Campground, go northeast on Forest Road 96. 2.0 miles - Stay left on Road 96, following the sign marked *Forest Hill Divide - Soda Springs - Foresthill.* Stay on the main road that winds in and out continually as it climbs up to the top of the ridge. (You will pass several forest roads that look worth exploring for future rides!) 5.6 miles - As you climb, look for a K-Tag (yellow sign) on a tree on the right that tells you your location is T15 North, R14 East, on the line between Sections 3 and 4. Just past the tag you will be treated to another outstanding view into Picayune Valley in Granite Chief Wilderness Area. 7.0 miles - You reach the top (7,180 ft.) after 1,850 feet of climbing. Enjoy the view of the volcanic rocks to your left (west). From the top, go left on Tevis Cup Trail, following the route of the Western States 100. The next 8 miles are all on challenging singletrack along Red Star Ridge. Don't think that it will be all downhill! Just like any ridge ride there are many great descents followed by some awesome climbs! You will gain a great respect for the runners who take part in the Western States Run! Most of this section of trail is rideable, but there are a couple of spots that almost everyone will have to push.

15 miles - At what appears to be the end of the ridge, turn right on the trail. Ride the short steep downhill and look straight ahead for

wooden signs on a tree: *Western States Trail - Robinsons Flat 6 miles.* For a longer stretch of singletrack, you could go right here (see Ride #4), but stay left to return to French Meadows. 15.3 miles - You reach another intersection with signs for the Western States Trail, Tevis Cup, Robinsons Flat, Poppy Campground, and a parking area. If you are tired, or tired of singletrack trail, go straight ahead to the parking area and turn left on the paved road. This will take you back to French Meadows Reservoir and your campground. If you would like a bit more adventure, go east (to the right as you face the Western States sign) and follow the signs to Poppy Campground. Taking this route, the trail connects with a road after 0.2 mile. Go left on the road for a short distance and then turn right on the trail marked McGuire Trail - Poppy Campground 2 miles. This short trail also ends on a road. Go left again and then right at the next intersection. Then follow the road until it ends.

You have to do a bit of hunting to find the McGuire Trail. Just remember to head downhill towards the lake the easiest way possible, and you will intersect the trail that follows closely along the lake shore. Be careful in the many creek drainages and watch out for hikers. This fun section is not too difficult, but it can be rough if you are exhausted. If you are tired, it's best to take the paved road option and save this trail for another day. 17.9 miles - Poppy Campground. 18.9 miles - The McGuire Trail ends on an old road. Go right and continue to McGuire Picnic Area. 19.2 miles - Go left when you reach the restrooms. There is a sign here that reads: *Trail to Western States - 3 miles to dam - 1 mile to Poppy Campground.* 19.7 miles - When you reach the main campground road turn right. 20.5 miles - When you reach Forest Road 96, turn left to return to Ahart Campground. Turn right if you are camped at French Meadows.

West Lake Bike Path at Tahoe

CHAPTER 8

🚲

Northwest Shore Lake Tahoe

The majority of rides in this chapter involve exhilarating climbs to mountains with views of Lake Tahoe and the peaks in Desolation Valley and Granite Chief Wilderness Areas. The rides start along the northwest shore of Lake Tahoe between Tahoma and Tahoe City, either from a campground or from a major road that is easy to find. If you are staying somewhere along the northwest shore you can ride the bike trail that runs along Highway 89 to get to the starting points

Campgrounds: William Kent, a 95-unit U.S. Forest Service campground, is located in the center of this area, with several other campgrounds nearby.

Seasons: June through October, or until the first snow falls!

Nearest Services: Small stores, gas stations and restaurants are located all along this stretch of Highway 89. If you can't find what you need, there are more stores in Tahoe City. Several bike shops are located between Homewood and Tahoe City. If you need more than a tube or a water bottle, look for a shop that does more than just rent bicycles. Some shops have mechanics available to help you with your questions and repairs.

WARD CREEK AREA

Trailhead Location: The rides in this section all begin at the William Kent USFS campground, T15N, R16E, Section 24.

Topo Maps: Tahoe City and Homewood 7.5 min., or Tahoe, CA 15 min.

Water: Treated water is available at the campground. There are streams along several of the rides, but you'll need to filter or treat the water.

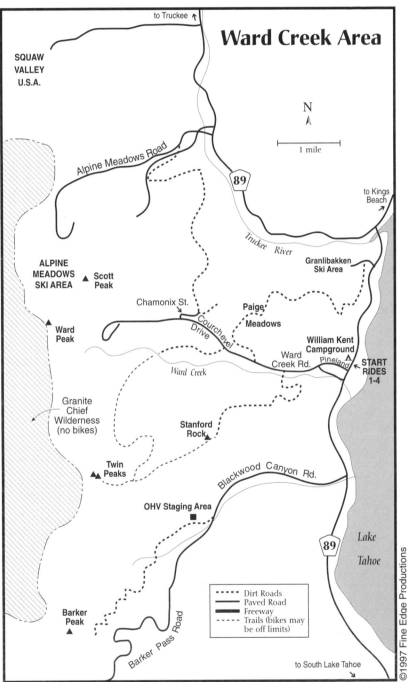

Ward Creek Area

to Truckee

SQUAW VALLEY U.S.A.

N

1 mile

Alpine Meadows Road

89

to Kings Beach

Truckee River

Granlibakken Ski Area

ALPINE MEADOWS SKI AREA

Scott Peak

Chamonix St.

Paige Meadows

Courchevel Drive

William Kent Campground

Ward Peak

Ward Creek Rd.

Pineland

START RIDES 1-4

Ward Creek

Granite Chief Wilderness (no bikes)

Stanford Rock

Twin Peaks

Blackwood Canyon Rd.

OHV Staging Area

89

Lake Tahoe

Barker Peak

Barker Pass Road

- - - - - Dirt Roads
———— Paved Road
▬▬▬ Freeway
– – – Trails (bikes may be off limits)

to South Lake Tahoe

©1997 Fine Edge Productions

#1   Ward Creek/Alpine Meadows Loop

Level of Difficulty: This is a fun ride for riders of all levels—a 21-mile spin! Beginners will find the distance a challenge, while more advanced riders will enjoy going for a mountain bike ride in Tahoe where you can actually spin your pedals the entire ride! A lot of fun, pure and simple—a nice break from all the hard-core climbing that many of the rides in the Tahoe area require.
Mileage: 21 miles with the run over to Paige Meadows, 16 miles without.
Elevation: 6,250 ft. to 7,200 ft.

0.0 mile - From William Kent Campground, ride south on the bike path that follows Highway 89. 0.3 mile - Turn right on Pineland Drive. The road is marked by two poles with "Pineland" carved into them. 0.7 mile - Turn left on Twin Peaks Road following the sign to Ward Valley. Stay on the main road, which turns right and becomes Ward Creek Road. Three miles out, the name of the road changes to Courchevel Drive. Continue on into the beginning of a subdivision on the backside of Alpine Meadows Ski Area.

3.3 miles - Turn right on Chamonix Street. At the end of the street, your dirt riding begins. Climb up a short hill, and then go right on the main road marked 16N48. 4.7 miles - After you cross a creek—which may be dry by the end of the summer—stay on the main road that goes left. (Another trail takes off to the right and ties into the road and trail system near Paige Meadows, where you will end up toward the end of this ride.) 6.2 miles - A gradual climb is now over, and you ride along and above the Truckee River Canyon. Look over your right shoulder to get a glimpse of Lake Tahoe. The road will turn west, taking you through an old ski area. The next section of old road is almost level, giving you a chance to relax and enjoy the view down into Alpine Meadows, with the peaks of Squaw Valley and the Granite Chief Wilderness in the distance. Soon the road drops steeply into the canyon.

7.8 miles - As you rapidly descend, the road makes a sharp right turn. Continue downhill. 8.2 miles - The dirt road ends at a USFS green gate. Go around the gate and continue down Snow Crest, a paved road. 8.6 miles - Turn right on Alpine Meadows Road. 9.5 miles - Turn right on Highway 89, and look off to the right side of the road for the start of the bike trail. The bike trail takes you along a beautiful section of the Truckee River, quiet and peaceful in the early spring or fall. If you do this ride in midsummer, however, the river may be bumper to bumper with rafts—and the trail just as crowded with hikers, joggers, skaters and cyclists.

13.3 miles - In Tahoe City, turn right staying on Highway 89, and go across the bridge, staying on the bike path. There are plenty of places to stop for snacks along here. If you've had enough just stay on the bike path 2.5 miles back to the campground for a 16-mile loop. To ride the longer loop, turn right at the sign to Granlibakken Ski Resort (14.0 miles). 14.3 miles - Turn left on Rawhide Road, just before the entrance to Granlibakken. Ride 0.2 mile to the end of Rawhide, where the road turns to dirt. 15.4 miles - Stay right on the main road that makes a sharp right turn and continues to climb gradually. There will be several junctions along the next part of the ride, but just stay on the main road that climbs gradually, then turns west and continues straight ahead.

17.0 miles - You arrive at one of the Paige Meadows. At the beginning of the meadow, the road is blocked off by a large log and the area is posted *No Motor Vehicles*. Go around the log and ride out to Paige Meadows. There are several trails through and around the meadows. Continue heading west on the trail that takes you from one meadow to the next, then turns into a road. 17.9 miles - Go straight and stay on the main road passing two roads on the right. Then get ready for a rocky downhill. 18.6 miles - Turn left on Ward Creek, the paved road. Follow it back to Pineland and down to Highway 89. Turn left to get back to the campground.

#2 Paige Meadows Loop

Level of Difficulty: This short ride is suitable for beginners and makes a perfect after-dinner ride for more advanced riders. (For a longer alternative, see Ride #1.)
Mileage: 10 miles.
Elevation: 6,250 ft. to 6,900 ft.

0.0 mile - From William Kent Campground, ride north on the bike trail along Highway 89. 2.0 miles - Turn left and follow the signs to Granlibakken Ski Resort. Just before you reach the resort turn left on Rawhide. Continue out until the road turns to dirt. 2.3 miles - Turn left on Rawhide Road just before the entrance to Granlibakken. Ride 0.2 mile to the end of Rawhide where the road turns to dirt. You will be riding next to private land, so be sure to stay on the main road. 4.4 miles - Stay right as the road makes a sharp turn and continues to climb gradually. There will be several roads taking off through the next part of the ride. Stay on the main road that climbs gradually and then turns west.

6.0 miles - You arrive at Paige Meadows. At the beginning of the first meadow, the road is blocked by a large log and the area is posted *No Motor Vehicles.* Go around the log and ride out to Paige Meadows. Paige Meadows is actually several large meadows clustered together. In early summer they will be bright green, and if you visit them in fall the meadows will be a golden brown (Ward Peak is in the background). Be sure to stay on the main trails when riding in this area. The meadows are starting to recover after what looks like years of jeep traffic driving wildly across them. There are several trails through and around the meadows. Continue following the main trail that goes west through the meadows, then turns into a road.

6.9 miles - After exploring the meadow trails, make your way over to the road. Go straight on the main road past two roads leaving to your right. After the rocky downhill, turn left on paved Ward Creek. 7.6 miles - Follow this road back to Pineland and down to Highway 89. Turn left and ride the bike trail back to the campground.

#3 Ward Creek

Level of Difficulty: Easy beginner ride. This is a good ride for a picnic along the creek. Beginners can rest at the creek while more adventurous riders can continue out the trail.
Mileage: 10.4 miles out and back.
Elevation: 6,250 ft. to 6,650 ft.

0.0 mile - William Kent Campground. Ride south 0.3 mile and turn right on Pineland Drive. 0.7 mile - Turn left on Twin Peaks Road and follow the sign to Ward Valley. Stay on the main road, which turns right and becomes Ward Creek Road. 2.2 miles - Turn left onto Upper Ward Creek (dirt road). After a short downhill it rolls along almost level to Upper Ward Creek. Several roads take off from the main road. Those to the right usually go back to the paved road, and the ones to the left go over towards Ward Creek and out into the meadow. 5.2 miles - The road ends at a *Road Closed* sign where the bridge across Ward Creek is gone. A trail continues on to the top of Twin Peaks from the other side of Ward Creek (see Ride #4). This ride ends here, so enjoy the creek and then follow your tracks back to the campground.

#4 Twin Peaks Bike and Hike

Level of Difficulty: Advanced level ride, suitable only for those looking for an adventure. Everyone will push or hike parts of this route, but at any point you can turn around and ride back down to Ward Creek.
Mileage: 16 miles out and back.
Elevation: 6,250 ft. to 8,878 ft.

0.0 mile - From William Kent Campground, follow the directions in Ride #3 the first 5.2 miles to Upper Ward Creek. 5.2 miles - Go around the *Road Closed* sign and cross the creek to continue by mountain bike up the trail to Twin Peaks. The route starts off as an old jeep road, then turns into a singletrack trail as it begins to climb up out of the valley. The trail is rough and suitable only for adventurous types, since it climbs about 1,900 feet in 2.6 miles. This may also be a ride where you choose to go as far as possible and then hide your bike for the final hike to the top of Twin Peaks. 7.8 miles - Once on top enjoy the view of Lake Tahoe to the east and Granite Chief Wilderness Area to the west. Hike back to where you left your bike and have fun on the downhill back to Ward Creek. On your way you may see another trail taking off

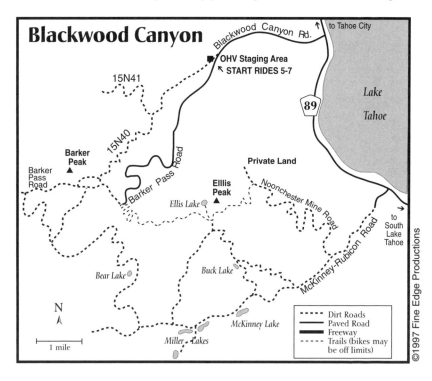

Blackwood Canyon

toward the ridge to the east. This is an alternate way down that will take you to Stafford Rock and a jeep road that returns to Ward Creek. (We never tried it, but we heard it was rideable.) Both downhill routes take you back to Ward Creek Road. Turn right and continue out to Highway 89. Turn left onto the bike trail to get back to the campground.

BLACKWOOD CANYON

The Blackwood Canyon OHV Area is the site of a large meadow restoration project. A gravel quarry in the past, it is now being returned to its natural state and is impressive—already wildflowers are returning!

Trailhead Location: Blackwood Canyon OHV Area, T14N, R16E, Section 34. To get to this area, ride or drive on Highway 89 to Kaspian Picnic and Bicycle Campground, just north of Tahoe Pines. Turn west on Blackwood Canyon Road (Road 03, 2 miles south of Pineland), which is marked with large SNO-PARK signs. Follow the signs to the OHV Area two miles out. Turn right on the gravel road into the OHV Staging Area, where you will find parking, restrooms and a picnic area. This is a good spot to start riding if you have a large group with many cars.

Topo Maps: Homewood and Wentworth Springs 7.5 min., or Tahoe and Granite Chief 15 min.

Water: Bring water with you; there is no treated water available in the Blackwood Canyon OHV Area. Stream water is available at Blackwood Canyon and Barker Creek out on the rides. Be sure to filter or treat all water from mountain streams.

From Blackwood Canyon OHV Area, everything is up. If you enjoy hill climbing, this is a good place for you to begin your rides which all start by climbing to the top of Barker Pass (7,700 ft.). Fortunately there are three options for getting there!

Option A: From the OHV Area, continue west on the 4-wheel drive road, 15N40. At 0.8 mile out the road splits. Continue riding straight ahead on 15N40. (The road to the right—15N41—climbs out of the canyon and ends 3 miles out.) As your road leaves Blackwood Canyon it gets rougher and steeper, with sections that many will have to push. This is a tough climb, but it is only 3 miles to the top. Once on top, the

Lake Tahoe Bike Rental

peak to the right (west) is Barker Peak, behind it is Granite Chief Wilderness Area, and to the left is Ellis Peak. From Barker Pass, turn left on Barker Pass Road for Rides #5 or #6, or turn right for Ride #7.

Option B: From the OHV Area, ride back out to the paved road, turn right, and ride up to the top of Barker Pass. With this option, it is 5 miles to the top, paved all the way and with a much more gradual climb. When the pavement ends, Ride #5 and #6 continue out on the trail to your left. To get to Ride #7 continue straight ahead 0.5 mile.

Option C: If you have more than one vehicle in your group, you can do a shuttle, leaving one car at Blackwood Canyon OHV and driving to the top of Barker Pass in the other.

#5   Ellis Peak Loop

Level of Difficulty: Strong intermediate or better. Most of this long all-day outing follows the route of the Tahoe Roubaix Race, known as one of the most challenging rides held in the Sierra. The elevation profile shows an overall gain of 2,000 feet, but because of terrain fluctuations you climb over 3,000 feet. The ride can be shortened and made easier by driving to the top of Barker Pass to start.
Mileage: 25 miles from the top of Barker Pass, or 29 miles if you start from Blackwood Canyon OHV Area.
Elevation: 6,400 ft. to 6,500 ft.

0.0 mile - From the Blackwood Canyon OHV Area, ride up road 15N40 to the top of Barker Pass. The mileage below assumes you chose to ride up 15N40 (Option A). If you use Options B or C, adjust your mileage accordingly. Add two miles if you ride the pavement, or subtract three miles if you drive to the top.

3.5 miles - Turn right on the motorcycle/hiking trail, which begins to climb immediately. If it hasn't rained in a while, the soil will be loose and most people will have to push through a series of switchbacks. Once on the ridge top, the trail becomes rideable again and you are treated to a magnificent view in all directions! The large lake to the southwest is Loon Lake, and if you look closely you will see Spider Lake and Buck Island Lake with Desolation Valley Wilderness Area in the distance. To the north is Blackwood Canyon, where you started your ride, and Lake Tahoe in the background.

5.5 miles - The trail ends at a road. To complete the loop, turn right. (If you take a left, you can ride out to Ellis Lake 0.5 mile for a swim.) 5.7 miles - Turn left. The road begins the final ascent to Ellis Peak. (Ride #6 goes straight ahead here.) 6.0 miles - Turn left. Ride as far as you can, then walk the final 0.1 miles to the top of Ellis Peak. Enjoy the view, then ride back down to the main road. 6.2 miles - Turn left. The road quickly becomes a trail and can be hard to follow. The trail you should be on stays on the north side of the ridge in front of you.

7.5 miles - When the trail ends at a dirt road, turn right on Noonchester Mine Road. This next section travels through private land, so be sure to stay on the road. Just after you cross Homewood Creek it's "heads-up" time: Be on the look out for a cable across the road! Negotiate the cable, then continue on. The road contours around the ridge, offering another great view of Lake Tahoe. Quail Lake is right below you. After you've enjoyed the view, prepare for the last three miles of wild downhill. *Warning! This next section of road is listed on the Tahoe Basin OHV handout, so be prepared for uphill traffic around every turn!*

10.5 miles - When you cross McKinney Creek, the downhill is over for a while. Turn right on McKinney-Rubicon Road. 11.8 miles - Continue straight ahead. (The steep road to the left goes to Buck Lake and then back up the hill to Ellis Peak). 13.0 miles - Off to your left is McKinney Lake. Continue on and pass by Lily Lake. Then the road begins to level out and you arrive at the first Miller Lake. 15.0 miles - Go straight past the second Miller Lake, where a road takes off to the left. This road goes to Richardson Lake and then down to Sugar Pine Point State Park. (For more information on rides to the south see *Mountain Biking the High Sierra, Guide 3A, Lake Tahoe South.*)

15.6 miles - Continue straight when a road enters from the right. (It is the road you come down in Ride #6.) 16.1 miles - Turn right when the road forks. (Left takes you out the Rubicon Jeep Trail that goes all the way to Loon Lake, an area also described in Guide 3A.) Climb to the top of the ridge and get ready for a fast downhill as the road circles around Bear Lake before climbing again.

20.5 miles - The road crosses Barker Creek. If you are out of water fill up here; there's one more climb to go. (Be sure to filter or treat the water). Ride across the creek, then take the road to the immediate right. It follows along Barker Meadows, through private land, and then to the final climb of the trip. 22.5 miles - You arrive back on top of Barker Pass. If you are tired, take the paved road back down to the OHV Area. If you want to ride more rough stuff, go across Barker Pass Road and take 15N40 instead.

#6   Miller Lake Loop

Level of Difficulty: Advanced level ride that climbs 1,800 feet and then descends on a fast, rough road. The views are spectacular!
Mileage: 20 miles (24 if you ride the paved road up to Barker Pass in both directions).
Elevation: 6,400 ft. to 8,200 ft.

0.0 mile - From the Blackwood Canyon OHV Area follow Ride #5 for the first 5.7 miles. 5.7 miles - Continue past the turnoff to Ellis Peak. Stay on the main road that starts downhill but levels off as you ride through a large meadow near North Miller Creek. If your hands are sore from squeezing the brakes, rest here; once you leave the meadow the road gets rough and drops steeply down to Miller Lake.

8.7 miles - The road ends at McKinney-Rubicon Road. Turn right. (Miller Lake is a short distance to the left.) 9.7 miles - The road forks.

Truckee River Bike Path

Truckee River Access Bike Trail parking lot

Turn right and begin climbing to the top of the ridge. Then it is time for a fast downhill as the road circles around Bear Lake before climbing again. 14.1 miles - You cross Barker Creek, then take the immediate road to the right. This follows along Barker Meadows (through private land) before you begin the final climb. 16.6 miles - You arrive back on top of Barker Pass. If you are tired, take the paved road down to the OHV Area, but if you want to ride more dirt, go across Barker Pass Road and take 15N40 instead.

#7   Barker Pass Loop

Level of Difficulty: Intermediate level ride. This is the easiest ride from Blackwood Canyon OHV Area, staying entirely on wide dirt roads, but there is still 1,300 feet of climbing.
Mileage: 12 miles (16 miles if you ride the pavement to and from Barker Pass).
Elevation: 6,400 ft. to 7,700 ft.

0.0 mile - From the Blackwood Canyon OHV Area, ride to the top of Barker Pass using any of the three options described in Ride #5. The mileage below assumes you chose to ride up 15N40, the dirt road. Be sure to adjust your mileage if you go up another way.

3.0 miles - From Barker Pass, ride across the main road and look for a road going down the other side. The Pacific Crest Trail also crosses here, but it is closed to bicycle use. Stay on the main road as it goes quickly downhill and levels out close to a meadow. Then follow along Barker Creek until the road ends at 5.0 miles. Turn right. The road begins to climb gradually at first, but it gets steeper as you work your way up into logging country. Logging roads take off at several places; stay on the main road with two wide switchbacks that take you back up to Barker Pass Road.

7.3 miles - Turn right on Barker Pass Road and ride back to Barker Pass. The rocky peaks to the southwest are in Desolation Wilderness Area, and Barker Peak is straight ahead. 8.6 miles - The shortest way down from Barker Pass is to take 15N40, the dirt road heading to the left. For a gentler descent stay on the main road which turns to pavement. Both take you back down to the OHV area.

PAVED BIKE TRAILS

Paved bike paths are on the increase in the Lake Tahoe area. These bike trails provide a great place for an afternoon spin, to get used to a bike, to ride with your children, to enjoy the scenery, and so on. Two very popular paths are located in the Tahoe City area, and they are both accessible from the Truckee River Access Bike Trail parking lot. The parking lot is located on the right (west) side of Highway 89, a quarter mile south of the "Y" (intersection of Highways 89 and 28) in Tahoe City.

Truckee River Bike Path

This trail, mentioned in the description for Ride #1, is probably the most popular bike path in the Lake Tahoe area. Since the entire length of the bike path follows the Truckee, it is a highly scenic trail.

From the parking lot, ride across the bridge to the north and go left on a wide, paved trail alongside the highway. The farther you get from town, the more interesting the forested surroundings become. The trail ends at 4.5 miles, and you turn around and head back to Tahoe City for a total of 9 miles on mostly flat terrain. To extend your ride, you can pick up the West Lake Bike Path described below.

West Lake Bike Path

From the parking lot, ride out toward Highway 89 and turn right (south) onto the paved trail. At 1.5 miles, the path crosses to the lake side of the road. At 1.75 miles, make a left turn down Sequoia toward Lake Tahoe, following the Bike Route signs. After Sequoia ends, you resume riding parallel to the highway. You cross the highway several more times—at 2.5, 3.25, and 5.25 miles. The paved bike trail ends at just over 5.5 miles. Unless you wish to ride on the highway for over a mile to find more paved bike path, turn around here for a total out-and-back ride of 11 miles. To extend your ride, you can add the Truckee River Bike Path described above for a total distance of 20 miles.

SQUAW VALLEY

Lake Tahoe's most famous winter sports area, Squaw Valley U.S.A., turns over its ski slopes to mountain bikers in the spring after the snow melts. Squaw Valley, which gained international recognition when it hosted the Winter Olympics in 1960, is located a few miles north of Tahoe City, just off Highway 89.

In the summer, Squaw Valley U.S.A. Mountain Bike Park offers many miles of singletrack, doubletrack, and roads, with trails for beginning, intermediate, and advanced riders. A cable car is available to take cyclists up to High Camp (8,200 feet). Information and rental bicycles may be obtained from the Squaw Valley Sport Shop, (916) 583-3356. While you are visiting, consider some of the other summer activities offered here, including swimming, horseback riding, bungee jumping, or a trip through the Olympic Museum.

CHAPTER 9

🚲

North Shore Lake Tahoe

This chapter has something for riders of all abilities: included are a ride to a secluded mountain lake, a lookout ride, a special section on riding the cross-country ski trails at Northstar Ski Area, and the Tahoe to Truckee Ride, route of one of the oldest mountain bike races held in the Sierra.

This is also timber country with endless miles of logging roads to explore. You will be riding through sections of private timber company lands, so always stay on the main roads and obey No Trespassing signs. Watch out for logging trucks.

Campgrounds: Several campgrounds are located nearby, and you can do the rides right from your campsite. The Tahoe State Recreation Area and Lake Forest are near Tahoe City. Along Highway 89 there are three U.S. Forest Service campgrounds: Granite Flat, Goose Meadow and Silver Creek.

Seasons: Mid-June through October.

Nearest Services: Tahoe City, Truckee and Kings Beach.

TAHOE TO TRUCKEE

#1   Tahoe City to Truckee

This ride follows the route of the Tahoe City to Truckee Race. For those who have never tried a mountain bike race and would like to, this is a good one to begin your career. Most of the route is on good surface dirt and gravel roads, with one small section of wide single-track. It is also used for running races, and in winter for cross-country ski racing.

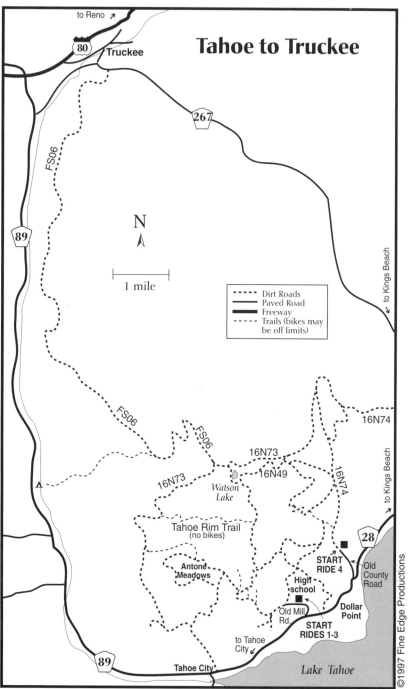

Tahoe to Truckee

to Reno

80 Truckee

267

FS06

89

N

1 mile

to Kings Beach

Dirt Roads
Paved Road
Freeway
Trails (bikes may
be off limits)

FS06

FS06

16N74

16N73

16N49

16N73

16N74

Watson
Lake

Tahoe Rim Trail
(no bikes)

to Kings Beach

28

Antone
Meadows

START
RIDE 4

Old
County
Road

High
school

Dollar
Point

Old Mill
Rd.

START
RIDES 1-3

to Tahoe
City

89 Tahoe City

Lake Tahoe

©1997 Fine Edge Productions

Level of Difficulty: Intermediate when ridden one way, but if you choose to do the entire 35+ miles out and back, you should be in very good shape and accustomed to riding all day. Most of the climbing is on good surface dirt roads; nothing too technical, but a very long ride.

Mileage: One way from Tahoe City (North Lake Tahoe High School) to Truckee (Thelin Drive) is 17.5 miles. If you ride one way from downtown Tahoe City to downtown Truckee, the total mileage is just over 22 miles. There is also the option of a 40-mile loop, in which you ride 19 miles on dirt and 21 miles on pavement.

Elevation: 6,250 ft. to 7,800 ft.

Water: Carry all you will need. Water is not available on the trail.

Topo Maps: Tahoe City and Truckee 7.5 min., or Truckee and Tahoe 15 min.

Trailhead Location: T16N, R17E, Section 3. Cyclists usually begin at North Lake Tahoe High School, but it is also convenient to start from the campgrounds and ride your bike to the school. Locals begin this run from numerous places, including a singletrack access at the Highlands Community Center. To reach the high school from the "Y" in Tahoe City (Highways 28/89 intersection), ride or drive northeast on Highway 28 through the main part of town. Turn left (northwest) on Old Mill Road, and after about a half mile, turn left again on Polaris at the top of the hill. Continue 0.4 mile farther to the end of the pavement just past North Lake Tahoe High School. If you drove to this point, park here out of the way of the school traffic.

Shuttle Parking: Most people prefer this route as a one-way ride with a car shuttle. A good place to leave your shuttle vehicle is where Forest Road 06 starts at Thelin Drive, or somewhere within the town of Truckee. (Truckee is usually full of tourists every day of the week during summer, and parking is at a premium in Old Town Truckee.) To get to Forest Road 06 from Truckee, drive southeast on Highway 267 and turn right on Palisades Road. Continue on until the road becomes Ponderosa Drive. Turn right on Silver Fir Drive and left onto Thelin Drive. Look off to your left for a green gate at the beginning of Forest Road 06. Park here without blocking the road.

0.0 mile - Ride out the dirt road that begins where the pavement ends at the entrance to Burton Creek State Park. Stay on the main road that leads through the forest and heads over towards Antone Meadows and Burton Creek. 0.3 mile - Stay left, then take an immediate right on the main road. 1.1 miles - Go straight, staying on the main road. 1.9 miles - When you arrive at a fork in the road, go right. You will be riding along the far edge of Antone Meadows. (The road to the left leads over to Antone Meadows and a small dam before it loops around and rejoins the road you are on.)

2.6 miles - At the upper end of the meadow, you ride through a big curve. Take the next right on a road that goes uphill, out of Burton

Creek State Park. As you leave the Park, the road turns into a wide singletrack trail and begins to climb. The singletrack climbs quickly and can sometimes be loose and difficult to ride. But if you hit it just after a thunder shower, the traction is great and the entire mile of singletrack is rideable. Be aware that this is a two-way road and you may encounter downhill traffic. Stay alert at all times! 3.6 miles - The singletrack ends in a switchback turn on Forest Road 16N73. Go right and continue climbing toward the top of Mt. Watson. 4.5 miles - The Tahoe Rim Trail crosses the road. 4.7 miles - Stay on the main road where another road takes off to the left. You pass a sign facing in the downhill direction: *Tahoe City 3 Miles.* 5.8 miles - As the road contours around the north side of the ridge, another road enters from the right. Go straight.

6.7 miles - You reach a junction, and are done with the majority of the climbing! Take a left here on Forest Road 06 and prepare for the

Tahoe's paved paths—share the trail

downhill section of the ride. (Straight ahead 6 miles is Brockway Summit on State Highway 267.) As you descend Forest Road 06, it stays wide and is not very technical. Just watch for gravel and sharp turns. Continue on this main road. This is logging country, so there are roads taking off all over the place. The main route is also a snowmobile and cross-country ski route, so you will see orange diamonds and snowmobile signs marked Forest Road 06. You ride along the boundary of Northstar Ski Area, then through a large plantation of trees. After 10+ miles of mostly downhill, the dirt road ends at a large gate.

17.5 miles - Turn left onto the paved road (Thelin Drive). You are now in a subdivision of Truckee. At the next intersection turn right on Silver Fir Drive. From here you can ride straight ahead on the pavement to get to downtown Truckee, or you can take a left on Aspenwood for a short singletrack down to town. If you choose Aspenwood, ride to the end of the pavement and continue out the rocky road. Just before the road reaches the power line, turn left down a trail. Go right at the next intersection and continue down the rocky trail. When you reach the edge of town, you can go left to Hill Top Restaurant, or go right to Pine Cone Drive. Either way, you need to continue downhill to the old part of Truckee and State Route 267.

To do this ride as a 40-mile loop, continue into town, cross the railroad tracks, and turn left. (*Watch out for tourists backing up their cars without looking!*) You might want to get off your bike and walk along the sidewalk for a bit of window shopping. If you are hungry or thirsty, you should have no problem satisfying those needs. Old Town Truckee is a fun place to explore if you have the time.

When you are ready to continue, you have two options. The first is to stay on the main road that crosses under Interstate 80 and goes through a newer section of Truckee. When you reach Highway 89, turn left and follow the signs to Tahoe City. The bike lane starts here. The other option is the dirt route that also brings you to the bike lane. For this, instead of staying on the main road, you ride the gravel road along the railroad tracks. When you reach the sign that reads *No Trespassing Beyond This Point*, turn right on the dirt road that goes up and over the hill. There are actually several roads that will work. Just remember to keep climbing. Then continue down the other side to where the dirt road ends at the intersection of Highway 89 and Interstate 80. Carefully cross the highway and turn left. You have now travelled 22 miles. If you are thirsty, you should probably stop here, because the next store is 9 miles farther.

Historic Truckee

For the next section of the ride, you travel on the bike lane along Highway 89, with a lot of traffic all the way to the Alpine Meadows turnoff. This can be incredibly noisy!

31 miles - You reach the turnoff to Squaw Valley, with a handy 7-11 store if you need a break from riding the pavement. 33 miles - From the turnoff to Alpine Meadows, the bike trail leaves the highway, and it is quite enjoyable to ride along the Truckee River. This is also a great route for people-watching, with many people riding along the bike path or floating down the Truckee River. 37 miles - The good bike trail ends at the intersection of Highway 89 and Highway 28. Turn left on Highway 28 and ride through Tahoe City. 39 miles - Turn left on Old Mill Road and ride the last uphill to your car at 40.0 miles.

#2 Antone Meadows Loop

Level of Difficulty: Easy beginner ride; also a perfect short ride for after dinner. Suitable for children and others new to mountain biking.
Mileage: 6.4 miles.
Elevation: 6,250 ft. to 6,840 ft.
Trailhead Location: North Lake Tahoe High School (see Ride #1 for directions).

0.0 mile - From North Lake Tahoe High School, ride out the dirt road that begins where the pavement ends. You will be entering Burton Creek State Park. Stay on the main road that leads through the forest and over toward Antone Meadows and Burton Creek. 0.3 miles - Stay left, then take an immediate right on the main road. 1.1 miles - Go straight, staying on the main road. 1.9 miles - When you arrive at a fork in the road (the road on which you 'll return), go right and ride along the far edge of Antone Meadows.

2.6 miles - You ride through a big curve at the upper end of the meadow. Stay on the main road that loops around the meadow. (Ride #1 takes off to the right from this point.) 4.3 miles - Turn left and continue to the dam on Burton Creek. If you do this ride in June or July, the wildflowers can be incredible! After exploring, continue on. 4.5 miles - You have completed the loop. Turn right and follow your tracks back to your car.

#3 Watson Lake Loop

Level of Difficulty: Strong beginner to easy intermediate.
Mileage: 17.5 miles.
Elevation: 6,250 ft. to 7,800 ft.
Comments: Watson Lake is a quiet spot most of the time, although the campsites look well used. We camped here one night and were amazed at how peaceful it was with the Tahoe summer traffic only 7 miles away! This is a great spot to camp and do some exploring. There are roads everywhere. If you decide to camp here, you need a campfire permit. For exploring, come equipped with a compass, topo maps, an OHV map and a Forest Service map. A helpful hint to remember is that, as a rule, most road numbers ending with 00 go somewhere, and the ones ending with a number like 05 and 13 are usually dead-end roads.
Trailhead Location: North Lake Tahoe High School (see Ride #1 for directions).

0.0 mile - From North Lake Tahoe High School, follow the directions given in Ride #1 to the intersection with Forest Road 06 and the main road to Truckee. 6.7 miles - Continue straight ahead on Road 16N73, Mt. Watson Road (6 miles to State Highway 267 at Brockway Summit). 7.0 miles - Turn right at a road marked by a stake with *6/30* on it. (This road is designated on OHV maps as Road 16N50). 7.6 miles - Watson Lake. Enjoy the solitude of the lake, take a swim and relax before continuing on. When you are ready to leave, follow the road that heads east away from the lake. After riding over a small hill, the road begins to descend rapidly. This is a rough and rocky downhill section. You pass a couple of roads that take off to the right, but stay on the main road.

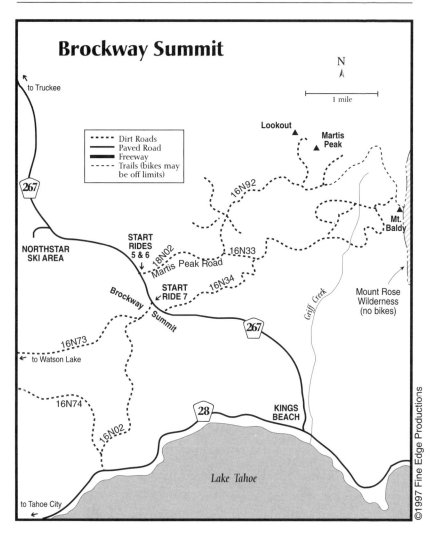

8.4 miles - Turn left on road 16N49. It heads through Watson Creek Meadow and then gradually climbs back to Mt. Watson Road (also know as 16N73 or Road 100). 8.8 miles - Turn left onto Mt. Watson Road. As it climbs back onto the ridge, be sure to look behind and to your left for a great view of Lake Tahoe. 10.8 miles - The Watson Lake Loop is complete and you are back at the intersection of Road 06. Continue straight ahead and follow your tracks back down to your car. *Caution: While you ride down the singletrack trail, watch out for uphill traffic!* (If you miss the turn onto the singletrack, 16N73 continues on and ends up in Tahoe City in a subdivision behind the golf course.)

#4   Watson Lake from Dollar Point

Level of Difficulty: Intermediate level ride with a good climb in the beginning.
Mileage: 13 miles, or 15 miles if you start in Tahoe City.
Elevation : 6,250 ft. to 7,800 ft.
Topo Maps: Tahoe City and Kings Beach 7.5 min., or Tahoe 15 min.
Trailhead Location: Ride or drive northeast on Highway 28, going 2.6 miles past
Tahoe City. Turn left on Old County Road at Dollar Point. Stay on Old County
Road until the pavement ends at Beverly Road, 0.8 mile farther. If you drove, park
your car here. Ride starts at T16N, R17E, Section 33.

0.0 mile - Ride out dirt road 16N74, located at the end of the pavement
to the right of a house. As you climb away from the lake, you pass
several roads entering from the left. Most of them are alternate routes
down from the top of the ridge. Just continue on the main road 16N74
to the top of the ridge. 3.2 miles -The road ends at Sawmill Flat. Turn
left on Mt. Watson Road 16N73, and continue to climb up the ridge to
Mt. Watson. In places it is steep and washboarded from logging trucks,
but it is still rideable.

4.7 miles - Forest Road 16N49 takes off to the left. This is the road
you will return on, but it is better to continue straight ahead and
get all of the climbing over first. 6.4 miles - Turn left at a road marked
6/30–16N50 on the OHV maps. (If you arrive at a major intersection
with Road 06, you went 0.3 miles too far.) 7.0 miles - Watson Lake.
When you are ready to continue, head east on the road that leaves the
lake. 7.8 miles - Turn left on road 16N49. This road goes through Watson
Creek Meadows and gradually climbs back to road 16N73. 8.2 miles -
Turn right on 16N73 and follow the tracks back to your car.

BROCKWAY SUMMIT

Riding in the Brockway Summit area is similar to the other spots around
Lake Tahoe in that all of the routes involve a fair amount of climbing.
But once on top, the rewards of spectacular views and exciting down-
hills make for wonderful riding terrain.

Trailhead Location: With the exception of Ride #8 (see specific direc-
tions in ride description), all rides described in this section start from
Brockway Summit on Highway 267 between Kings Beach and Truckee.
From Kings Beach—on the north shore of Lake Tahoe—drive north on
Highway 267 to the top of Brockway Summit. As you start down the
east side, look off to your right (north) for dirt road 18N02. Park here

or drive in a bit if you want to shorten the rides and cut down on the amount of climbing you will do. Rides start at T16N, R17E, Section 3.
Topo Maps: Martis Peak and Mt. Rose 7.5 min., or Truckee and Mt. Rose 15 min.
Seasons: June through October.
Nearest Services: Kings Beach.

#5   Martis Peak Lookout

Level of Difficulty: Suitable for intermediates and those who enjoy a good climb. Like most lookout rides, it's up on the way in and down on the way back out.
Mileage: 6 miles out and back.
Elevation: 7,150 ft. to 8,656 ft.
Water: Bring all that you will need; many of the creeks will be dry by midsummer.

0.0 mile - From Highway 267, ride out road 18N02. Stay on the main road that climbs steep at first and then becomes a more gradual climb. (The main roads in this area are marked with cross-country ski diamonds for winter use.) 1.3 miles - Go left on the main road. (The road

Approaching rainstorm

straight ahead is 16N33.) 1.9 miles - At a five-way intersection, stay on the main road that continues to climb. 3.3 miles - The road reaches the ridge top. Take a left here to finish the final climb to the lookout tower.

3.9 miles - Martis Peak Lookout (elev. 8,656 ft.) To the north are Donner Lake, Prosser Lake, Boca Reservoirs and Dry Lake. To the south you can see all of Lake Tahoe! To the west is Mt. Watson, Mt. Pluto and Northstar Ski Area. For a better view to the east, ride or walk the final 100 feet to the top of Martis Peak. When you are done enjoying the view, prepare for the wild descent and follow your tracks back to your car. (For a longer ride, turn left, instead of right, at the first intersection and follow the directions for Ride #6 below.)

#6   Mt. Baldy Loop

Level of Difficulty: Strong intermediate or advanced, due to the amount of climbing and the singletrack. This ride can be done in both directions, and it is hard to say which way the climb is easiest or the downhill more fun.
Mileage: 12.6 miles.
Elevation: 7,150 ft. to 9,100 ft.
Water: Bring all that you will need, since many of the creeks will be dry by midsummer.

0.0 mile - Start at road 18N02 on Highway 267. Follow Ride #5, Martis Peak Lookout, for the first 3.3 miles. Continue straight ahead instead of turning left to go to the lookout. 3.9 miles (0.6 mile from the lookout intersection) - Take an old jeep road off to the right (more like a trail than a road). There is a rock painted lavender in the middle of the trail, and orange flagging hanging in a tree at the start. Follow this old road all the time. You may have to push in spots. 4.7 miles - At a fork, go right and continue climbing and pushing to the top of the first ridge. 5.2 miles - The trail becomes a jeep road and stays fairly level for a short while, then it begins to climb. 6.6 miles - Stay left, continuing the climb up the ridge.

6.8 miles - Turn left here to go to the top of Mt. Baldy for another great view of Lake Tahoe. (This is the intersection you will be returning to after climbing to the top.) 7.2 miles - Look off to the left for a yellow sign (a "K-tag") on a tree that marks the boundary between California and Nevada. Welcome to Nevada! 7.3 miles - Lay down your bike, and hike out to the edge to enjoy the 360° view! When you are ready to ride again, return to the last intersection 0.4 mile back. (Ride

Hilly singletrack

#7 continues on from the top.)

7.7 miles - Turn left at the intersection this time and prepare for a long downhill stretch. Stay left on the main road past the first four junctions. At times you will feel like you are losing too much elevation and that you are going to end up in Lake Tahoe, but don't worry—you can enjoy over 2 miles of downhill before you need to turn. From the map, it appears that other roads to the right will also take you back to the Martis Peak Lookout Road. Just be careful, because this is one of those places with roads going everywhere! 10.5 miles - Turn right. The road flattens out before climbing just a bit. 11.3 miles - Road 16N33 ends at the Martis Peak Road. Stay on the main road to return to your car.

#8   Watson Lake from Brockway Summit

Level of Difficulty: Beginner ride. All on wide dirt or gravel roads.
Mileage: 11.5 miles out and back.
Elevation: 7,200 ft. to 7,800 ft.
Water: None available; carry all that you will need.
Topo Maps: Tahoe City and Kings Beach 7.5 min., or Tahoe and Truckee 15 min.
Trailhead Location: This ride starts on the Mt. Watson Road (16N73), a dirt road that goes west from the top of Brockway Summit. (Also see the Tahoe to Truckee map, p. 114).

0.0 mile - Ride southwest on Mt. Watson Road. It is primarily gravel and climbs 600 feet right at the beginning, but it is not a difficult road to ride. 2.7 miles - You reach Sawmill Flats and Forest Road 16N74. Continue straight ahead and climb up the ridge toward Mt. Watson. It is steep in places and washboarded from logging truck traffic, but it is still rideable. 4.2 miles - Forest Road 16N49 takes off to the left. This is the road you will return on, but you may as well continue straight ahead and get all of the climbing over first.

5.9 miles - Turn left at the road marked *6/30*, which is designated 16N50 on the OHV maps. (If you arrive at a major intersection with Road 06, you went 0.3 miles too far.) 6.5 miles - Watson Lake. When you are ready to continue, head east on the road that leaves the lake. 7.3 miles - Turn left on road 16N49, which goes through Watson Creek Meadows and gradually climbs back to 16N73. 8.2 miles - Turn right on 16N73 and follow your tracks back to the car.

NORTHSTAR SKI AREA

When you are planning a trip to North Tahoe, another spot worth checking out is Northstar Ski Area, located just off Highway 267 between Kings Beach and Truckee. Northstar is a year-round recreation area with downhill and cross-country skiing in winter, and a wide variety of summer activities such as tennis, rock climbing, horseback riding, swimming, hiking and mountain biking. The cross-country ski trails are open to mountain bikes, and from these trails there is good access to the surrounding National Forest. Riding from Northstar, you can tie into the road system near Mt. Watson. Cyclists of all skill levels will find suitable rides at Northstar!

When you arrive at the main village center at Northstar, you should check at the Mountain Adventure Shop for trail maps and information on which trails are currently open or closed to riders. The shop rents a variety of mountain bikes, offers daily introductory mountain bike lessons, and has information about other events it sponsors (guided lunch tours, shuttles to the top of the mountain, and Mountain Bike Weekend packages). For more information, call the Mountain Adventure Shop at (916) 562-2248.

CHAPTER 10

🚲

Northeast Shore
Lake Tahoe

The rides described in this chapter are located on the east side of Lake Tahoe in the mountains known as the Carson Range. Compared to the Sierra on the western side of the lake, the climate is much more arid, with fewer densely forested areas and more high alpine sage groundcover.

The main highways here are State Route 28 along the northeast shore of Lake Tahoe, Mt. Rose Highway (431) connecting Incline Village to Reno, and Highway 50, to the south.

One section of this chapter is devoted to Spooner Lake State Park, where you will find the route description for one of the most well-known rides in the western United States, The Great Flume Ride– a "must do" for those with intermediate or better riding skills. The route is a challenge, and the views are incredible!

Campgrounds: The only campgrounds in this area are located on the Mt. Rose Highway. Bike-in and wilderness campsites are available in Spooner Lake State Park. Other than the wilderness campsites, the State Park is for day-use only.

Seasons: June through October–spectacular in the fall! The east side of the Sierra has large aspen groves which turn bright yellow to orange around the first of October.

Cruisin'

127

Nearest Services: Incline Village or South Lake Tahoe will probably have everything you need in the way of food, restaurants, lodging and bike shops.

SPOONER SUMMIT

To get to Spooner Summit from South Lake Tahoe, drive northeast on U.S. 50 about 12 miles past the casinos and turn left onto Nevada State Highway 28. Continue north for about a half mile before turning right into Spooner Lake State Park. (From the North Shore of Lake Tahoe, take Nevada State Highway 28 south from Incline Village. Just before the junction of Highway 28 and U.S. 50, turn left into the State Park.

Spooner Lake State Park is a day-use facility, and it is certainly worth the $4 entry fee to park your car inside ($1 fee if you enter by bike). This area is currently closed to motor vehicles (except park vehicles), including motorcycles, and there have been rumors of possibly closing it to mountain bikes. Injured people who can't ride out have to be evacuated by park personnel, and unfortunately this happens several times each summer. Also, many riders park outside the gate and ride in without paying. Money is spent on the park's trail system to maintain it for everyone, and mountain bikers need to pay their fair share. If you choose to ride in this area, please do your part and pay the $4 so others will have the chance to ride here in the future.

This State Park is rich in history. The Spooner Lake area was used by the Washoe Indians as a camp, and during the 1870s it was a central point in the route for transporting wood from Glenbrook (on the shore of Lake Tahoe) to Virginia City. If you are interested in local history, pick up a brochure when you enter the park.

Trailhead Location: All rides in this section start from within the picnic area at Spooner Lake at T14N, R18E, Section 12.
Topo Maps: Marlette Lake, Glenbrook 7.5 min., or Carson City 15 min.

#1   Marlette Lake

Level of Difficulty: Strong beginner to intermediate. If you are unsure whether or not you can do the Flume Ride you should plan to do this one first as a trial.
Mileage: 12.5 miles out and back.
Elevation: 7,000 ft. to 8,157 ft.

0.0 mile - Go east out of the picnic area toward Spooner Lake. Turn left (north) on the dirt road that heads toward the big meadow. The road continues along North Canyon Creek and the edge of the meadow. It then begins climbing up towards Marlette Lake, passing an old cattle grazers cabin built in the 1920s. 2.8 miles - You reach the first of the backcountry campgrounds. Continue straight ahead. 3.9 miles - Continue straight ahead to go to Marlette Lake. To the right is road 15N04A, which takes you to the top of Snow Valley Peak (elev. 9,214 ft.) after 1.5 miles of climbing. It's a steep, steady climb with an incredible view from the top!

4.2 miles - At elevation 8,157 feet, the climbing is over! Enjoy the 0.6 mile descent to Marlette Lake. When you arrive, turn left and follow the road that goes around the shore. Marlette Lake is used as a breeding area for cutthroat trout, and there is a small hatchery at the inlet on the south end of the lake. No fishing is allowed. 6.2 miles - You arrive at the dam. (A left turn would take you on the Flume Ride.) This ride ends here, so rest and enjoy the view before following your tracks back. *Caution: Be sure to ride carefully down the hill! Be on the lookout for hikers, horseback riders, and cyclists making their way up. The turns can be loose and sandy, so control your speed at all times!*

#2   The Great Flume Ride

This is one of the true "classic" Tahoe rides, a technical ride with magnificent views the entire way. It has been pictured and described in virtually every national mountain magazine! You ride singletrack trail on the abandoned flume line that follows the east side of Lake Tahoe, a thousand vertical feet above the lake.

Level of Difficulty: Strong intermediate or better; a technical ride, this is only for those with prior trail riding experience. Done as a loop, with ample time to enjoy the scenery, the ride takes most cyclists all day to complete.
Mileage: 23 miles.
Elevation: 7,000 ft. to 8,300 ft.
Water: Good water is available in the Picnic Area at Spooner Lake. There are several spots along the way to get water from creeks and lakes, but it must be filtered or treated.

0.0 mile - Starting from Spooner Lake Picnic Area go north on the dirt road (North Canyon Road), following the directions for Ride #1 to

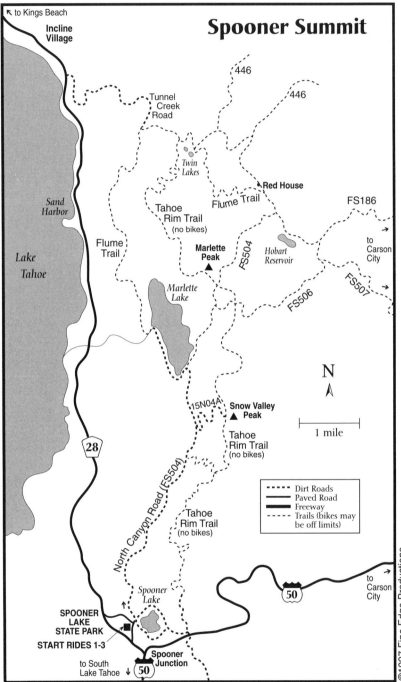

Spooner Summit

to Kings Beach

Incline
Village

446

446

Tunnel
Creek
Road

*Twin
Lakes*

Red House

Flume Trail

FS186

Tahoe
Rim Trail
(no bikes)

*Sand
Harbor*

Marlette
Peak ▲

FS504

Hobart
Reservoir

to
Carson
City

FS507

*Lake
Tahoe*

Flume
Trail

*Marlette
Lake*

FS506

15N04A

Snow Valley
▲ Peak

N

Tahoe
Rim Trail
(no bikes)

1 mile

28

North Canyon Road (FS504)

Tahoe
Rim Trail
(no bikes)

········ Dirt Roads
———— Paved Road
━━━━ Freeway
‑ ‑ ‑ ‑ Trails (bikes may
          be off limits)

*Spooner
Lake*

50

to
Carson
City

SPOONER
LAKE
STATE PARK

START RIDES 1-3

Spooner
Junction

to South
Lake Tahoe ↓ 50

Marlette Lake. Continue to the dam. 6.2 miles - Look off to the left end of the dam (southeast) for the sign: *Flume Trail.* Carefully ride down a short, steep, sandy stretch with a sharp right turn at the bottom. Continue across Marlette Creek and you will encounter the Flume Trail. It is a narrow trail contouring along the ridge at 7,700 feet, 1,500 vertical feet above Lake Tahoe! *Caution: Do not attempt this trail if you are afraid of heights or have not done much trail riding with your bike!* The trail is not that difficult, but it is not a beginner ride either! For the next 4.5 miles you will be following the route of a flume (water system), originally developed in the 1870s to deliver water around the ridge to help transport logs and water to Virginia City. In places you will still see the pipes which replaced the original wooden flume. Be careful–they can be slippery at times. Plan on enough time to enjoy the views along the way, and if you like to take pictures bring along a camera. This is the place to take unbelievable photos of your friends riding along rugged granite walls with Lake Tahoe and the surrounding mountains in the background.

10.6 miles (4.5 miles of single track later!) - The Flume Trail ends at Tunnel Creek Road. The road to the left continues down 3 miles to Hidden Beach on Highway 28. Just below this spot, down Tunnel Creek Road, are the remains of a tunnel that was blasted 4,000 feet through the mountains to the eastern side; water was transported through it by another series of flumes.

For a shorter ride than 23 miles, many mountain bikers ride down Tunnel Creek Road to waiting shuttle vehicles parked along Highway 28 (a total ride of 13.7 miles), and then drive back to Spooner Lake State Park. To continue on the loop ride, however, turn right and ride up to the top of the ridge. 11.1 miles - The road to Twin Lakes takes off to the right. The Lakes are about a half mile away. Continue straight, or detour to the lakes before continuing on. 11.8 miles (0.7 mile past Twin Lakes sign) - While you are heading down the dirt road, look to your right for another section of rideable Flume Trail. The most enjoyable way is to turn right and continue along the flume, so look carefully. If you miss this turn, don't worry; continue down the road and take the next main road to the right. It will take you past the "Red House" and connect again with the Flume Trail. (The Red House is one of the old flume tender's houses built in 1910.)

Follow the Flume Trail as it contours around the east side of the Carson Range. Watch out for downed trees. Some of them you can ride over, others you can ride under, and some you will have to portage around. 14.2 miles - The Flume Trail ends at a small diversion dam. Carefully walk across or around the dam and continue up to the main road. Turn right. 14.7 miles - Turn right on Forest Road (504) that soon crosses Franktown Creek. If you need water, get it here. (Be sure to filter or treat the water.) The next section is a one-mile uphill that is mostly in the sun. Take a rest if you need it, then begin the climb to the top of the ridge. 15.9 miles - You have reached the top! Continue

The Flume Trail

on out the ridge.

16.3 miles - The road forks. Although it may seem like it is time to go downhill, continue straight ahead. After a bit more ridge riding, the road quickly descends to Marlette Lake. 19 miles - You are now back at Marlette Lake and have completed the Loop part of the ride. Turn left at the intersection following the signs back to Spooner Summit. After a short climb, it's time for 4 miles of downhill. This section can get quite wild—sand seems to be in all the turns! Be sure to watch out for hikers, horseback riders and other cyclists. *Stay on the right side of the road and control your speed at all times.* It's 23 miles back to Spooner Lake and your car.

#3   Hobart Reservoir Loop

Level of Difficulty: Intermediate ride, all on dirt roads.
Mileage: 20 miles.
Elevation: 7,000 ft. to 8,300 ft.

0.0 mile - From Spooner Lake, ride north on the road to Marlette Lake, following the directions in Ride #1. 4.8 miles - Turn right when you reach the lake (the Flume Ride goes left here) and ride along the southeast shore. The road to Hobart Reservoir climbs a bit, follows the ridge line and descends the eastern side into a meadow and across Franktown Creek. 7.5 miles - Turn right and continue 0.5 mile to Hobart Reservoir. Hobart Reservoir is the main water supply for Virginia City, Silver City, Gold Hill and parts of Carson City, amazing when you look on the map to see just how far away Virginia City is!

8.6 miles - Stay to the right. 0.3 mile farther, stay right again. The two roads you pass are the eastern access routes to this area if you are coming from Carson City or the Washoe Lake area. Continue on Forest Road 506, which turns west and begins to climb over Carson Ridge. 13.0 miles - After a short downhill you return to the road you started on. Turn left and ride down the hill to Marlette Lake. 14.8 miles - At Marlette Lake turn left, ride up the hill, then enjoy the downhill back to your car. *Caution: Be sure to ride carefully down the hill! Be on the lookout for hikers, horseback riders, and other cyclists making their way up. The turns can be loose and sandy, so control your speed at all times!*

MT. ROSE HIGHWAY

To get to these rides, start from Incline Village and either ride or drive

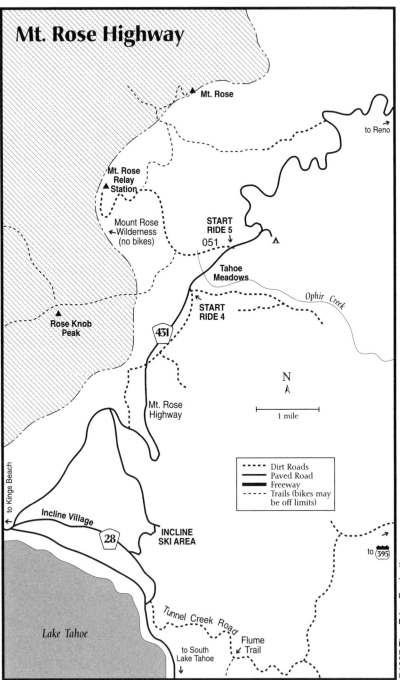

Mt. Rose Highway

▲ Mt. Rose

to Reno →

▲ Mt. Rose Relay Station

Mount Rose
← Wilderness
(no bikes)

START RIDE 5
051

Tahoe Meadows

Ophir Creek

START RIDE 4

▲ Rose Knob Peak

431

N

1 mile

Mt. Rose Highway

- - - - Dirt Roads
——— Paved Road
███ Freeway
- - - Trails (bikes may be off limits)

to Kings Beach ←

Incline Village

28

INCLINE SKI AREA

to 395

Lake Tahoe

Tunnel Creek Road

to South Lake Tahoe ↓

Flume Trail

©1997 Fine Edge Productions

north on Highway 431. If you are staying in Incline Village, you may choose to ride your bike from town. If so, look off to the side of the road after you leave the subdivisions for the old Mt. Rose Highway; ride it instead of the new road.

#4   Ophir Creek Trail

Level of Difficulty: Good for beginners and children. This is a pretty spot, with limited riding and is probably not worth a special trip. But if you are on your way to Reno, or you like little out-of-the-way spots where you can ride, picnic, hike and go fishing, give Ophir Creek a try. Ophir Creek looks small, but while it is only two to three feet across, it is three feet deep with even deeper holes! People were fishing successfully while we were here, and the creek looks crystal clear.

Mileage: Ophir Creek Trail is 3 miles out and back; from Incline Village 17 miles.

Elevation: 8,500 ft. with very little elevation gain. If you choose to start this ride from Incline Village and ride up to the trail, the elevation gain will be from 6,240 feet to 8,500 feet.

Campgrounds: Mt. Rose Campground is located 10 miles up Highway 431—almost to the summit. According to the Campground Host, this USFS campground is rarely full, except on the busiest weekends of the summer. The terrain is fairly barren, although there is a creek nearby.

Topo Maps: Mt. Rose 7.5 min., or Mt. Rose, NV 15 min.

Trailhead Location: Ophir Creek Trailhead, T17N, R19, Section 36. Drive or ride up Highway 431, which travels northeast out of Incline Village 7.5 miles. Off to your right (east) is the Ophir Creek Trailhead sign. The trail is located on the edge of Tahoe Meadows, a large, flat expanse with a winter parking area. If you come to the parking area you have gone too far, so head back to the edge of the meadow by the creek to find the trail. Park at the trailhead.

Follow the "trail"–really an old jeep road–out about a mile and a half. Several short out-and-back options are also available. This is a large winter recreation area with cross-country ski markers on many trees. Just before the road ends, you will see another road taking off down a drainage. This old 4-wheel drive road turns into a motorcycle trail and then ends up at Incline Village Ski Resort. If you decide to follow this down, please obey all signs and stay on the trail - you are travelling through private land. A short distance past Incline Ski Area, you reach a large intersection where three roads meet. Turn right. Follow this road back to Highway 431, find the old Mt. Rose Highway, and ride back up to your car or continue straight ahead to Incline Village.

#5   Mt. Rose Relay Station

Level of Difficulty: Advanced ride, due to the elevation and lack of shade.
Mileage: 8 miles out and back.
Elevation: 8,800 ft. to 10,160 ft.
Water: None available; carry all that you will need.
Seasons: Mid-June through October. Avoid the middle of summer, since there is no shade on this ride.
Trailhead Location: Driving northeast on Highway 431 from Incline Village, you'll see a gated road 1 mile past Tahoe Meadows on the left. Park here, or drive up to Mt. Rose summit to park.

This ride takes you to the top of a 10,166-foot peak with a Relay Station (Radio Repeater and Microwave Station) at the top. Don't be fooled by the low mileage! This is a tough climb, similar to riding up to fire lookouts. 0.0 mile - Ride your bike out the 4-wheel drive road marked *Forest Road 051.* Stay on the main road that climbs up and around a ridge, then turns north into a canyon. 2.2 miles - (Note: At this point, the trail to the left goes to Gray Lake; the trail to the right goes to Mt. Rose. Although you may hike to either of these destinations, *your bike is not allowed in the Wilderness.)* Continue on to the relay station. The road begins to get very steep as you climb the final 80 ft. to the top. 3.9 miles - You're at the top now where you have a spectacular 360° view. When you have enjoyed the view retrace the route back to your car.

Beautiful Lake Tahoe

APPENDIX

IMBA Rules of the Trail©

The International Mountain Bicycling Association's Rules of the Trail have been recognized by the U.S. Forest Service, Bureau of Land Management, the Sierra Club, and the International Cycling Union—the world governing body of bicycle racing. These rules apply wherever you ride, including ski areas.

1. Ride on open trails only. Respect trail and road closures (ask if not sure), avoid possible trespass on private land, obtain permits and authorization as may be required. Federal and State wilderness areas are closed to cycling. Additional trails may be closed because of sensitive environmental concerns or conflicts with other users. Your riding example will determine what is closed to all cyclists!

2. Leave no trace. Be sensitive to the dirt beneath you. Even on open trails, you should not ride under conditions where you will leave evidence of your passing, such as on certain soils shortly after a rain. Observe the different types of soils and trail construction; practice low-impact cycling. This also means staying on the trail and not creating any new ones. Be sure to pack out at least as much as you pack in.

3. Control your bicycle! Inattention for even a second can cause disaster. Excessive speed maims and threatens people; there is no excuse for it!

4. Always yield trail. Make known your approach well in advance. A friendly greeting or bell is considerate and works well; startling someone may cause loss of trail access. Show your respect when passing others by slowing or even stopping. Anticipate that other trail users may be around corners or in blind spots.

5. Never spook animals. All animals are startled by an unannounced approach, a sudden movement, or a loud noise. This can be dangerous for you, others, and the animals. Give animals extra room and time to adjust to you. In passing, use special care and follow the directions of horseback riders (ask if uncertain). Running cattle and disturbing wild animals is a serious offense. Leave gates as you found them or as marked.

6. Plan ahead. Know your equipment, your ability, and the area in which you are riding, and prepare accordingly. Be self-sufficient at all times, keep your machine in good repair, and carry necessary supplies for changes in weather or other conditions. A well-executed trip is a satisfaction to you and not a burden or offense to others. Keep trails open by setting an example of responsible cycling for all mountain bicyclists.

Rules of the Trail ©1988 by International Mountain Bicycling Association (IMBA) may be used for public education purposes with the following credit given:

Dedicated to the appreciation of and access to recreational lands, non-profit IMBA welcomes your support. IMBA is a non-profit advocacy organization that promotes mountain biking that is environmentally sound and socially responsible. IMBA educates mountain bikers, helps government officials promote the sport through innovative management techniques, sets a positive image for off-road cycling, promotes volunteer trail work, and keeps trails open and in good condition for everyone. To join IMBA or receive additional information, call 303/545-9011 or write IMBA, P.O. Box 7578, Boulder, CO 80306.

Mountain Bike Associations for the North Lake Tahoe Area

These volunteer nonprofit organizations need your help:

Tahoe Area Mountain Bicycling Association (TAMBA)
P.O. Box 1488, Tahoe City, CA 95730   (916) 525-5100

Tahoe Rim Trail
P.O. Box 10156, South Lake Tahoe, CA 96158

International Mountain Bicycling Association (IMBA)
P.O. Box 7578, Boulder, CO 80306-7578   (303) 545-9011

The Care and Feeding of a Mountain Bike
BY R. W. MISKIMINS

ROUTINE CHECKUPS FOR YOUR BICYCLE

The key to years of fun and fitness from your mountain bike is giving it checkups on a regular basis. You need to know how to clean it, lubricate a few places, make simple adjustments, and recognize when something needs expert attention. For the average rider, most bike shops recommend tuneups once a year and complete overhauls every two to three years. All of the maintenance in between your trips to the bike shop you can do yourself. Given below is a nine-step checkup procedure–a list to run through after every extensive ride–before you head back out into the hills again.

1. CLEANUP
Unless the frame is really filthy, use a soft rag and a non-corrosive wax/polish such as Pledge to wipe off the grime and bring the old shine back. If you need to use water or soap and water prior to the polish, don't high-pressure spray directly at any of the bearing areas (pedals, hubs, bottom bracket or head set). You should clean all your components, too (including the chain and the rear cogs), but use a different rag and a lubricant such as Tri-Flow or Finish Line for wiping them down. Do not use polish or lubricants to clean your rims–an oily film will reduce your braking ability. Instead, wipe off the rims with a clean dry rag. If you need to remove rubber deposits from the sidewalls of the rims use acetone as a solvent.

2. INSPECTION
After you get the grit and grime off, check out the frame very carefully, looking for bulges or cracks. If there are chips or scratches that expose bare metal (especially when the metal is steel), use automotive or bicycle touch-up paint to cover them up. Your inspection should also include the components. Look for broken, bent or otherwise visibly damaged parts. Pay special attention to the wheels. When you spin them, watch the rim where it passes the brake pads. Look for wobbles and hops, and if there is a lot of movement, the wheel needs to be trued at home (or take it to a bike shop) before using it. Look for loose or broken spokes. And finally, carefully check your tires for sidewall

damage, heavy tread wear, cuts and bulges, glass and nails, thorns, or whatever.

3. BRAKES

Grab the brakes and make sure they don't feel mushy and that the pads are contacting the rim firmly (be certain the brake pads do not rub against the tires!). If the brakes don't feel firm, there are barrel adjusters at one or both ends of the wire cables that control the brakes–turn them counterclockwise to take up some of the slack. If you are unsure as to the dependability of your brakes, for safety's sake let a bike shop check them.

4. BEARING AREAS

Most cyclists depend upon professional mechanics to fix any problems in the pedals, hubs, bottom bracket or head set, but they should be able to recognize when something is wrong. Spin the wheels, spin the crankarms (and the pedals) and move the handlebars from side to side. If you feel notches or grittiness, or if you hear snapping, grating or clicking noises, you have a problem. Check to make sure each of the four areas is properly tightened. To check for looseness, try to wiggle a crankarm side to side or try to move a wheel side to side. Check your headset adjustment by holding the front brake, rocking the bike forward and backward, and listening for clunking sounds.

5. SHIFTING

Presuming your bike has gears, check to make sure you can use all of them. The most common problem is the stretching of the inner wire that operates the rear derailleur. If your bike is not shifting properly, try turning the barrel adjuster, located where the cable comes out of the derailleur. Turn it just a little; usually a counterclockwise direction is what you need. Unless you know what you are doing, avoid turning the little adjustment screws on the derailleurs.

6. NUTS AND BOLTS

Make sure the nuts and bolts which hold everything together are tight. The handlebars and stem should not move around under pressure, and neither should your saddle. And make certain that the axle nuts or quick-releases that hold your wheels are fully secure–when a wheel falls off, the result is almost always crashtime. If you have quick-release hubs, they operate as follows: Mostly tighten them by holding the nut and winding the lever, but finish the job by swinging the lever over like a clamp (it's spring-loaded). Do not wind them up super tight as you would with a wingnut—for safe operation they must be clamped, and clamped very securely, with considerable spring tension! If you are at all uncertain regarding the use of quick-releases, go by a bike shop and ask for a demonstration.

7. ACCESSORIES

Make sure all your accessories, from water bottles to bags to pumps to lights, are operational and secure. Systematically check them all out and if you carry flat-fixing or other on-the-road repair materials or tools, make sure you've got what you need and you know how to use what you carry. Statistics show that over 90% of all bicycle breakdowns are the result of flat tires, so it is recommended that you carry a pump, a spare tube, a patch kit, and a couple of tire levers with you whenever you ride.

8. LUBRICATION

The key to long-term mechanical happiness for you and your bike is proper and frequent lubrication. The most important area of lubrication is the chain—spray it with a Teflon-based or other synthetic oil (WD-40, household oil, and motor oil are not recommended), then wipe off all the excess. You can use the same lubricant for very sparsely coating the moving parts of your brakes and derailleurs.

9. INFLATION

You now are ready for the last step. Improper inflation can lead to blowouts or pinch flats. Read the side of your tires to see what the recommended pressure is and fill them up. If there is a range of pressures given, use the high figure for street cycling, the low figure or near it for off-road riding.

After going through these nine steps of getting your bike ready you've earned another good long ride!

Basic Skills for Mountain Biking
BY R. W. MISKIMINS

Everybody knows how to ride a bike—at least almost everybody can ride around the neighborhood. But with the advent of the mountain bike, riding a two-wheel pedal-powered machine has gotten more complicated. Watch a pro-level mountain bike race and the need for "technical skills" will become obvious. Can you handle steep hills, big rocks, creeks, muddy bogs, loose sand, big tree roots, deep gravel, or radical washboards? These are the kinds of factors that differentiate mountain biking from road riding and that demand skills and balance above and beyond those required to ride around the neighborhood. The key to acquiring these abilities is practice—start easy and work diligently until you achieve high-level control of your bike.

1. BICYCLE

All mountain bikes are not created equal. Some are better suited to staying on pavement. They have too much weight, too long a wheelbase, ineffective braking systems, sloppy shifting, too smooth tread on the tires, poorly welded frames, and so on. As a general rule, the mountain bicycles marketed by the discount store chains, department stores, and sporting goods stores are only suited to on-road, non-abusive use. Bicycles from bike stores, excepting their least expensive models, are generally suited to heavy duty, skilled off-road use. They should be relatively light (under 30 pounds), and have a fairly short wheelbase and chainstay (for agility), moderately steep head angle (again for agility), strong and dependable braking and shifting systems, well-made frames, and knobby/aggressive tires.

For details on choosing the right bike for you, consult the experts at your local bike shop. They can help you not only with selecting a bicycle, but also with various accessory decisions, in such areas as suspension forks, bar ends, and gear ratio changes. And of extreme importance, whatever bike you decide on, get the right size for you. If a bike is too big for your height and weight, no matter how hard you try, you will never be able to properly handle it. If you are in doubt or in between sizes, for serious off-road riding opt for the smaller bike.

2. FUNDAMENTAL PRINCIPLES

There are some very general rules for off-road riding that apply all the time. The first, "ride in control," is fundamental to everything else. Balance is the key to keeping a bike upright—when you get out of control you will lose your ability to balance the bike (that is, you'll crash). Control is directly related to speed, and excessive speed for the conditions you are facing is the precursor to loss of control. When in doubt, slow down!

The second principle for off-road riding is "read the trail ahead." In order to have time to react to changes in the trail surface and to obstacles, you should be looking ahead 10 to 15 feet. Especially as your speed increases, you want to avoid being surprised by hazardous trail features (rocks, logs, roots, ruts, and so on)—if you see them well ahead, you can pick a line to miss them, slow down to negotiate them, or even stop to walk over or around them.

The third principle is to "stay easy on the grips." One of the most common reactions by novices in tough terrain is to severely tense up, most noticeably in a "death grip" on the handlebars. This level of tightness not only leads to hand, arm and shoulder discomfort but interferes with fluid, supple handling of the bike. Grip loosely and bend at the elbows a bit—don't fight the bicycle, work with it!

The last general principle to be presented here is "plan your shifting." If you are looking ahead on the trail, there should be no shifting surprises. Anticipate hills, especially steep ascents, and shift before your drive-train comes under a strong load. Mountain bikes have a lot of gears and their proper use will make any excursion more enjoyable.

3. CLIMBING

Mountain bikes were originally single-speed, balloon-tire cruisers taken by truck or car to the top of a hill and then used for exciting and rapid descent. After a few years, they were given gears to eliminate the shuttle. Today's off-road bikes have 18 to 24 speeds, with a few extremely low gears so they can climb very steep hills. One of the keys to long or difficult climbs is attitude; it's a mental thing. You need to be able to accept an extended, aerobic challenge with the thoughts "I can do it" and, above all, "This is fun."

Your bike is made with hill-climbing in mind. Find a gear and a pace that is tolerable (not anaerobic) and try to maintain it. Pick a line ahead, stay relaxed, and anticipate shifting, as noted earlier. In addition, be alert to problems in weight distribution that occur when climbing. It is best to stay seated, keeping your weight solidly over the traction (rear) wheel if possible. However, if the slope is so steep that the front wheel lifts off of the ground, you will have to lean forward and slide toward the front of the saddle. Constant attention to weight distribution will give you optimum traction and balance for a climb. And make sure your saddle height is positioned so when your foot is at the bottom of a pedal stroke, your knee is very slightly bent–a saddle too low or too high will significantly reduce both power and control on a steep and difficult climb.

4. DESCENDING

This is where most serious accidents occur, primarily because a downhill lends itself to high speed. It is unquestionably the most exciting part of mountain bike riding–expert riders reach speeds over 60 mph! For descents, the "stay in control" and "read the trail ahead" principles can be injury-saving. Know your ability and don't exceed it. And be certain your brakes are in good working order–don't believe the slogan "brakes are for sissies." On steep and difficult downhills everyone has to use them. Regarding braking, always apply the rear brake before the front (to avoid an "endo"–that is, flying over the handlebars), and if possible, brake in spurts rather than "dragging" them. On easy hills, practice using your brakes to get comfortable with them.

As was the case for steep uphills, steep descents require attention to weight distribution. Many riders lower their saddle an inch or two prior to descending (to get a lower center of gravity). All cyclists quickly learn to lift their weight slightly off the saddle and shift it back a few inches to keep traction and to avoid the feeling of being on the verge of catapulting over the handlebars. Practice this weight transfer on smooth but steep downhills so you can do it comfortably later on obstacle-laden terrain. Finally, it is possible to go too slow on a difficult downhill, so slow you can't "blast" over obstacles. Instead, because of lack of momentum, hazards can bring you to an abrupt stop or twist your front wheel, and both of these results can cause loss of control.

5. TURNING

A particularly treacherous time for mountain bikers is high speed or obstacle-laden turns. The first principle is: don't enter a curve too fast. Turns often contain loose dirt and debris created by all the mountain bikes that preceded you. Slow down before you get there; you can always accelerate during the turn if you choose. Lean around the turn as smoothly as possible, always keeping an eye out for obstacles. It is common for the rear wheel to skid in turns. To take the fright out of that phenomenon, go find a gentle turn with soft dirt and practice skidding to learn how you and your bike will respond.

6. OBSTACLES

If you get into the real spirit of off-road cycling, you will not ride just on smooth, groomed trails. You will encounter rocks, roots, limbs, logs, trenches, ruts, washboards, loose sand (or dirt or gravel), and water in a variety of forms from snow and ice to mud bogs to free-flowing springs and creeks. Obviously, the easiest means for handling an obstacle is to go around it; however, you can't always do that. For raised obstacles, those you need to get up and over, riders need to learn to "pop the front wheel." To practice this, find a low curb or set out a 4x4 piece of lumber. Approach it, and just before the front wheel impacts it, rapidly push down then pull up the front wheel. The wheel lift is enhanced if you simultaneously lower and raise your torso and apply a hard pedal stroke. After your front wheel clears the obstacle, shift your weight up and forward a little so the rear wheel can bounce over it lightly.

If you encounter "washboards," the key to relatively painless negotiating is to maintain a moderate speed and get into a shock absorbing posture–slightly up and off the saddle, knees slightly bent, elbows slightly bent, loose grip on the handlebars, and relaxed. Soft spots in the trail can make your bike difficult to control and create an instant slowdown. If you have to deal with loose, deep sand, dirt or gravel, the key is to go slower but "power through." Shift your weight back a little (for better traction), then keep your bike straight and keep pedaling. Maintaining momentum and a straight line is also important in mud holes; be certain to do any shifting prior to soft spots or muddy bogs (otherwise you will lose momentum). Sharp turns can present a particular problem in these conditions–you will be much more prone to losing the rear wheel to a slide out, so be extra cautious in sandy or muddy curves.

Going through water can be a lot of fun, or it can be a rude awakening if you find yourself upsidedown on a cold February afternoon. Before any attempt to cross a waterway, stop and examine it first. Make sure it isn't so deep that it will abruptly stop you, then find the route that has the fewest obstacles (look for deep holes, big rocks, and deep sand). Approach the crossing at a fairly low speed and plan on pedaling through it (rather than coasting) for maximum traction and control. Be aware of the potential for harmful effects that riding through water can have on your bearings (if they are not sealed) and exposed moving parts. Plan on lubricating your chain, derailleurs, inner wires, and so on, when you return home. Finally, regarding snow and ice, stay away from it as much as possible. Snow riding can be fun but if it's deep, it can be very laborious. Maintaining momentum and avoiding buried obstacles are the two major tasks for snow riders. Also, the difficulty of steep ascents and descents are significantly magnified by a few inches of snow. Most mountain bikers riding on snow prefer flat or nearly flat terrain.

Roadside Repairs
BY R. W. MISKIMINS

Cyclists who take a little time to prepare for equipment failure before riding will get the most enjoyment out of their bicycle. Although there are dozens of things that can go wrong on a ride, especially if you crash, most of them happen so rarely that it doesn't make a lot of sense to worry about them. The chance that you will need to replace a bent axle or replace a wheel with a dozen broken spokes or tighten the lock ring on your cassette (rear sprockets) or replace a defective shift lever is always there, but thankfully these are not the common trailside problems. For these kinds of difficulties, most cyclists ride, carry or coast the bike back to their car, any way they can, and head for a bike shop.

It has been written that more than 95% of all trailside or road-side repairs involve either fixing flats or simply tightening something that has rattled loose. With this in mind, consider the following as insurance against long walks home.

PRE-RIDE PROTECTION
Bicycles arrive from the factory with regular tubes and no added protection to cut down on the possibility of flats. There are three different approaches to minimizing the possibility of air loss while riding your bicycle. The most popular over the years has been "thorn resistant" tubes (they used to be called "thorn proof"). They do help, but are not very effective against much of what might create problems for you. Two more effective products are tire liners (plastic or Kevlar and plastic strips that go inside the tire, between the tire and the tube) and sealants (goo that goes inside the tube and seals the holes that thorns, staples, and so on make). Some cyclists employ two and sometimes three of these measures to minimize flat tires. Bear in mind that each of them adds a significant amount of weight to your bike, so it is best to select one and hope for the best. Short of using solid, airless tubes (which is not recommended), nothing is foolproof. Always be prepared to fix flats.

BICYCLE BAGS
Whatever you choose to carry in the form of tools and spare parts will

require a comfortable means to haul them. Although you could carry what you need in a fanny pack or backpack or even in your pockets, the most popular kinds of bike bags are those that fit under the rear of your saddle (underseat bags). They do not interfere with mounting or dismounting or handling and they carry a remarkable amount of gear. The best ones have some form of plastic clips, rather than just straps, to attach them to the bike. The extremely small ones are best suited to racing since they carry very little. The extremely big ones are best suited to slow, nonaggressive riding; they tend to bounce around on rough terrain and, when full, add too much weight. Other forms of bags include the frame pack, which doubles as a shoulder strap when carrying your bike; handlebar bags, which are suitable when off-road handling is not an issue; and bags that attach to racks (either on top or hanging down alongside the wheel), which are most often used for long-distance touring.

REPAIR KIT

Author Ray Miskimins

Once you have chosen a bag for your bike, consider the following as essentials to put in it: a spare tube (whenever possible, put patches on punctured tubes at home rather than in the outback), a patch kit to cover you if you get more than one flat on an outing, tire levers (plastic tools for getting the tire off and back on the wheel), and a set of Allen wrenches—especially 4mm, 5mm and 6mm—to tighten up loose stem, saddle, handlebar, shifters, and so on. Be certain, before you go riding, that you know how to take your wheels on and off and how to replace a bad tube. A lot of people carry the right repair materials but don't know how to use them.

These suggestions will take care of a remarkable number of trail/road repairs. At many shops this is all that is recommended for the typical cyclist to carry. There are a few other tools, however, that some cyclists—especially mountain bikers who ride far from civilization—like to carry. Again, if you bring these tools along, be sure they will work for your specific bike and that you know how to use them.

Consider the following possibilities: crescent wrench (needed if both your wheels are not quick release), chain tool to repair damage to the chain by taking out a link or two, spoke wrench for straightening slightly bent wheels, crank wrench for tightening loose crankarms, small screwdriver for derailleur adjustments, cone wrench for tightening loose hubs, or socket wrenches (8mm, 9mm, or 10mm) to use for brake adjustments and the like. In addition, some long-distance cyclists carry spare parts such as cables, brake pads, and a rag to wipe their hands.

BICYCLE PUMPS

Since flat tires are the primary problem for cyclists, a pump becomes important. It doesn't do any good to replace a punctured tube with a new one if you cannot inflate it. There are basically three kinds of bicycle pumps.

Floor pumps are generally too awkward to carry on a ride; but since they pump high volumes of air and fill tires rapidly, they are perfect for home and shop use.

For many years, most cyclists have carried frame-fit pumps on their bikes for emergency use. With the proper size they can be squeeze-fit on to a bicycle frame with no additional hardware needed. If you use a frame-fit pump on a mountain bike and you like to ride rough terrain, however, consider a secondary velcro tie or something similar to ensure that the pump doesn't fly off the bike as you negotiate bumps. Also, consider placing the frame-fit pump behind your seat tube rather than in the usual position below the top tube, so it is not in the way if you need to carry your bike.

Mini-pumps, the third type, have become most popular for mountain bikers over the past few years. They are very small and can fit into out-of-the-way places on your bike, such as alongside a water bottle cage. This requires special hardware, but it is a very tidy application. The down side to these pumps is that they move very small volumes of air at a time. Many of them now are "double shot," meaning they move air when both pushed and pulled. Since pumps are for emergencies, inflating a tube beats hours of walking, no matter what size your pump.

Finally, be aware that there are two different kinds of valve stems on bicycles now. The "regular" ones, like those on cars, are called Schrader valves. The skinny metal ones are Presta valves or French valves, and they require that you first unscrew the little gadget on the top before applying a pump. All the standard pumps now can be altered to work for either type of valve. Also available at a very nominal cost are adaptors that allow you to use Presta valves at a regular gas station pump connection.

Below is a checklist for the most basic, inexpensive roadside repairs:

[ ] tire liners   [ ] patch kit   [ ] mini pump
[ ] underseat bag   [ ] tire levers   [ ] Allen wrenches
[ ] spare tube   [ ] Presta adaptor
                            (if needed for your bike)

First Aid
BY RÉANNE DOUGLASS

Several years ago on a mountain biking trip, I miscalculated a sharp turn on a sandy stretch of dirt road, went flying, and turned my right shin into raw meat. I didn't have a first aid kit with me. Why bother? After all, I was cycling off-road, no traffic around, and I planned to be gone just part of the day.

When I got home, I took a shower, cleaned my wound, and applied some antibiotic cream. Three days later, however, Don had to carry me to the doctor. A staph infection—that took three pain-filled weeks to control—had set in.

Don't be careless like I was. Carry and use a first aid kit. You can purchase one at a bike shop or sporting goods store, or you can make your own.

For day rides, we suggest the following items:

8 Bandaids 1" x 3"	8 gauze pads, 3" x 3"
6 antiseptic swabs or	8 aspirin tablets or substitute
1 oz. hydrogen peroxide	4 antacid tablets
1 roll adhesive tape	1 elastic bandage
1 moleskin 3" x 4"	1 needle
1 single-edge razor blade	waterproof matches (in film can)
sunscreen, 15 SPF or better	prescription medicines (if applicable)

Index of Rides and Riding Areas